WRESTLING
IN
AKRON

FRONT COVER: Don Eagle, the darling of Ohio fans, delivers a dropkick to an unidentified opponent in an Akron match. He enjoyed a spectacular professional career but could not conquer private matters outside the ring and ultimately committed suicide. (Courtesy Jason Sanderson.)

COVER BACKGROUND: "Whipper" Billy Watson of Canada used Toronto as his home base but made many trips into Ohio, both during his stint as world champion and when he was only a contender to the throne. He was a charismatic performer with a vast arsenal of moves to use against all corners. (Courtesy Jason Sanderson)

BACK COVER: Dr. Jerry Graham (far left) poses with a group of wrestlers in California late in his career, after wearing out his welcome in the Midwest. Though always a top draw in the Ohio area, Graham's personal demons were too much to handle, leading to problems both in and out of the ring. After varied "no shows" and brushes with the law, promoters started regarding him as too big of a liability, in spite of his worth at the gate. No longer able to get bookings in the East or Midwest, he headed westward for his last hurrah, as seen here.

WRESTLING IN AKRON

Dale Pierce

ARCADIA PUBLISHING

ISBN 978-1-4671-1017-4

Published by Arcadia Publishing
Charleston, South Carolina

Printed in the United States of America

Library of Congress Control Number: 2013931051

For all general information, please contact Arcadia Publishing:
Telephone 843-853-2070
Fax 843-853-0044
E-mail sales@arcadiapublishing.com
For customer service and orders:
Toll-Free 1-888-313-2665

Visit us on the Internet at www.arcadiapublishing.com

I dedicate this project to my wife, Denise, as well as to all the warriors of the squared circle and the mat who made their mark in the Akron area.

CONTENTS

ACKNOWLEDGMENTS

All photographs are by the author or from the author's collection unless otherwise stated. Other contributors include Tina Mucciolo, Jason Sanderson, Acme Archive, Bob Crumby Collectibles, Tony Lanza Archives, Summit County Library, Bruce Kettlewell, Cleveland Public Library, Paige Von Hess Sutherland, Mike Lano, and others as noted.

INTRODUCTION

Akron, Ohio, has a rich and colorful past. The All-American Soap Box Derby, the rubber industry, the railroading ties, and a number of now defunct amusement parks all make up a glorious history that has been covered elsewhere. What has not been dealt with too often, however, is the area's long-standing love for wrestling, both in professional and amateur forms.

From the seedy days of traveling carnivals and clandestine fights with onlookers making bets in back alleys to actions drawing thousands in major venues, wrestling was always an attraction. Maybe the people of Akron just liked or still like a good fight. Who knows? In any case, the idea of watching men and women do battle with each other has been a passion the locals have long embraced.

Traditionally, the era of the Akron Armory remains the Golden Age for wrestling historians. There were plenty of matches held before this building was completed in 1918 and, of course, lots of action after it was closed to contests in 1976. It was then torn down in 1982. After housing decades of shows and playing host to a number of greats, the arena did have one final hurrah when the wrestling movie *All the Marbles* included some scenes of the armory.

There were a few other venues holding wrestling during the armory's reign, including an Eagles lodge and some dance halls, but it was this 3,000-seat structure that became the embodiment of Akron wrestling for what seemed an eternity.

The armory died, but wrestling lived on. There were the promotional wars between the National Wrestling Alliance (NWA) and World Wrestling Federation (WWF), with the latter finally winning out, only to abandon Akron as a monthly stop afterward. There was the emergence of many independent groups who came and went, while others survive to this day, running in smaller venues.

The names from the past that came to Akron reads like an honor roll for pro wrestling. Johnny Powers, Don Kent, Hans Schabel, the Sheik, Pampero Firpo, Lou Thesz, Kurt Von Hess, Marvin Mercer, Abdullah the Butcher, Buddy Rogers, Hank James, Primo Carnera, Bobo Brazil, and Dizzy Davis were just some of the notables who ventured into the area. They were the good. They were the bad. Sometimes, they were the ugly. No matter what the case or individual brand of in-ring mayhem, they always entertained.

The faces and places haves changed. Greats from times gone by have been replaced by new stars. The Mighty Jebediah, Jessicka Havok, Durty the Clown, and a host of regional personalities now keep the sport alive, while an infrequent spot show done by a major cable-based promotion still swings by on occasion. In any case, pro wrestling lives on.

Aside from the pros, with their weird antics, posturing, and outlandish televised interviews, there is also the flip side for wrestling in Akron in the form of amateurs. The high schools, community colleges, and, of course, University of Akron all offer their brand of wrestling on the mat. They, too, need to be remembered.

The more things change, the more they remain the same. Professional wrestling has evolved over the decades from traveling sideshow circuits and occasional contests held irregularly in major cities, to high-gloss cable television shows seen around the globe and wrestlers catapulted to true superstar status. Yet, in spite of the evolutionary points, the general concept of good versus evil and smiling fan favorites (known in the inside jargon as "baby faces") fighting an endless onslaught of heels, or bad guys, has been a game plan held to for ages.

1

THE EARLY YEARS

The earliest pro wrestling in Akron and environs came in two forms, both of which would seem shadowy by modern standards. Yet, from these dubious beginnings, the traditional style developed with bad guys fighting good in various venues.

First were the illegal fights arranged in alleys, warehouses, and railroad yards. Serbian, Croatian, and Italian immigrants who came to Akron to work the railroads or rubber factories were particularly enthusiastic for this form of combat, though the clandestine brawls attracted all ethnic groups, with bets being places on the combatants

Likewise, traveling carnivals passing through town had their local wrestlers accepting challenges from members of the audience or, in some cases, prearranged plants, where bets were again taken on the outcome of the matchups. Suspiciously, most endings for the encounters went against the way the bets leaned, so the promoter cleaned up, then moved on to the next town before people realized they had been taken to the cleaners.

From the heart of these dubious practices emerged modern professional wrestling, and with the coming of the Akron Armory, such spectacles would find a longtime home.

Rough and tumble bare-knuckle boxer John L. Sullivan served as a prototype for loads of carnival wrestlers, back-alley prizefighters, and even pro wrestlers in the decades to follow. Though originally a hard-drinking and even harder-living man in his prime, Sullivan became a teetotaler in later years, speaking against the demons of alcohol. Many carnival wrestlers and boxers imitated not only his style, but also his image, with close cropped hair and a handlebar mustache.

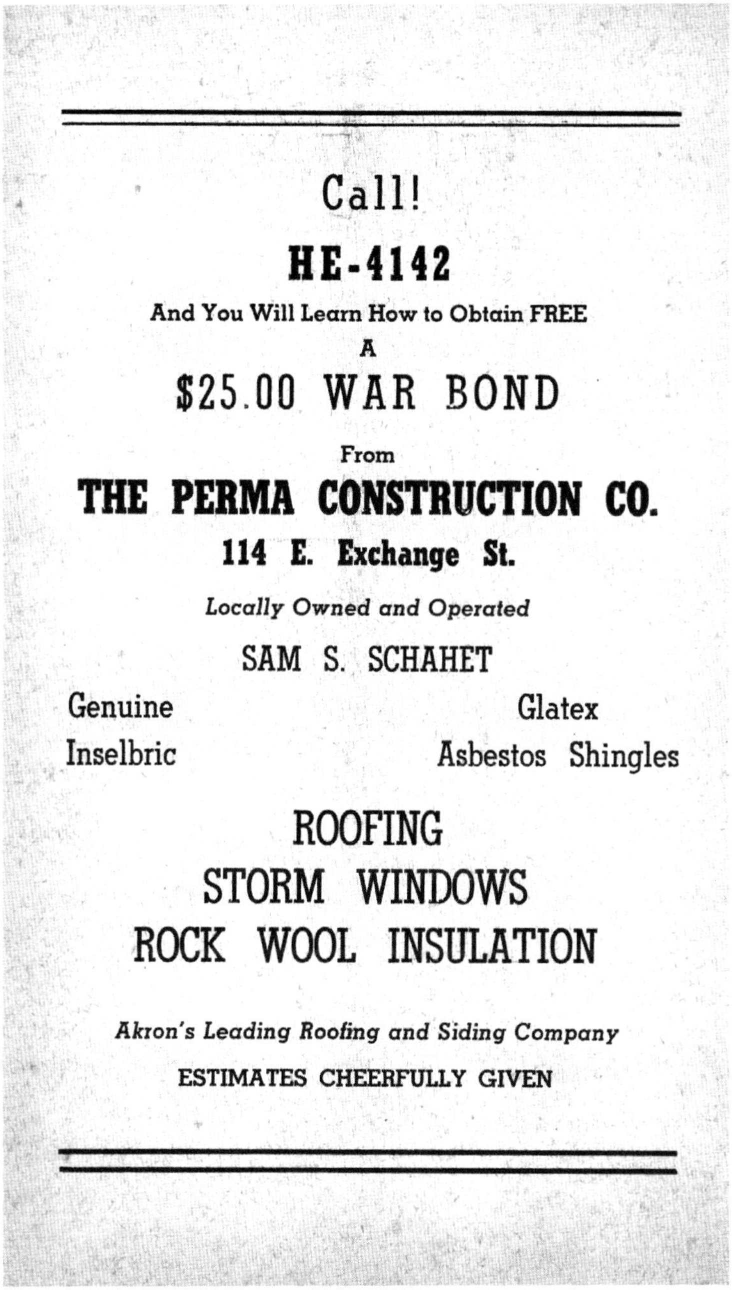

Akron was said to be in the running for a title match between Frank Gotch and Tom Jenkins in 1903, but Cleveland won out instead, as it was considered the home base for Jenkins. Jenkins, in fact, won this encounter in an upset but lost a return match to Gotch, again in Cleveland, in 1905. This was the first true attempt to bring major stars to Northern Ohio. A trend would develop with future promoters suing the draw from these shows as a learning mechanism. They developed regular venues, found sponsors for advertisements in programs (such as the one here), and built wrestling in a continual attraction.

A group of Serbian immigrants pose for a family picture after moving to Akron. The Serbians and other migrant groups loved to watch fighting, including underground contests with heavy betting.

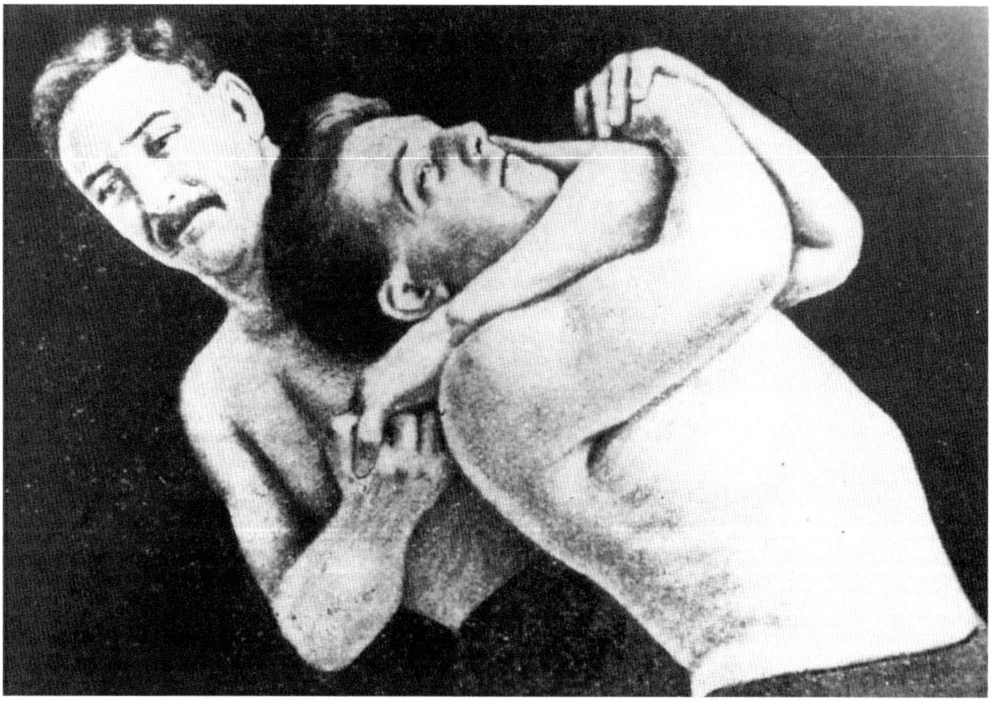

Farmer Burns made the rounds throughout the Midwest, not only wrestling but also demonstrating a talent many outlaws would have loved to have had: the ability to be hanged with a noose, while tightening his neck muscles so the rope had no ill effect on him.

Aside from freak shows, midways, wrestling attractions, and other oddities dating back to the 1880s, carnivals also offered photo opportunities, such as these pony photographs taken in Akron in the 1930s.

The goat cart was also a popular draw for kids at many carnival attractions, while tent shows attracted the adults. Carnival owners were slick operators who sought to make money by any and all means necessary. Families and children were a focal point, as were single patrons.

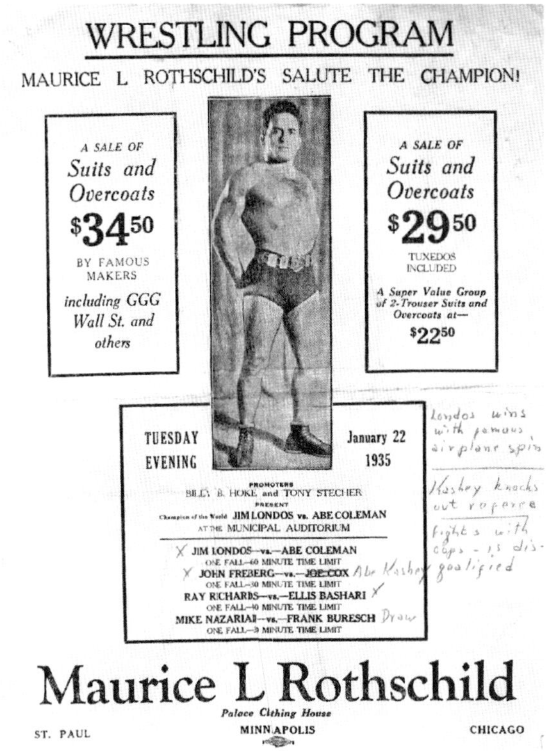

This image depicts a 1933 Chicago program featuring long-standing world champion Jim Londos. During his lengthy career, Londos also appeared regularly in Ohio, with Akron, Columbus, Mansfield, Marion, and Canton being some of his stops. He eventually retired to California, where he owned a farm until his death in 1975. On February 11, 1918, Londos beat Charlie Flashcamp in Akron and won a rematch on March 21 as well.

An alligator wrestler demonstrates his art form in a traveling carnival. Pro wrestler and animal trainer Tuffy Truesdale, better known for teaching bears to wrestle, did the same as an added attraction at an actual Akron Armory card, where he subdued a live alligator before a stunned crowd.

Jova Copa served as a referee in the early days of Ohio wrestling. A migrant worker from Serbia, he found extra cash as an arbitrator of fights, though he is seen here posed in his Sunday best and not dressed for refereeing.

An interior shot from a wedding reception photograph depicts some of the design within the Fraternal Order of Eagles lodge hall, which also served as a location for occasional wrestling shows starring Tex Hager, Monte Ladue, Earl Malone, and others.

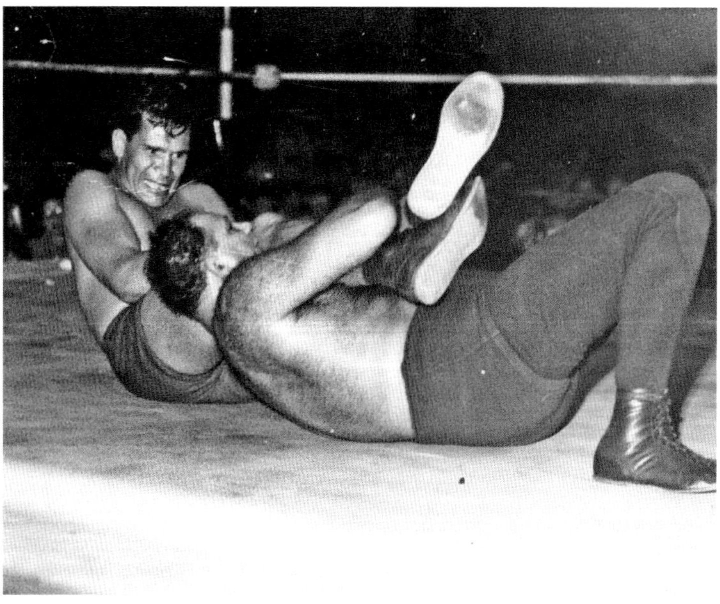

This image was captured during a wrestling match at the Eagles lodge in Akron in the 1940s. The lodge hall never housed matches on a continual basis, but it served as an occasional location for spot shows featuring an odd combination of regional wrestlers and big stars. (Courtesy Jason Sanderson.)

This aging carnival barker was still hanging on with the circuit in the 1930s. Carnival workers and wrestlers spoke a quasi-language of their own called "carnie," in which they inserted an "iz" after the first consonant in each word, enabling them to communicate with each other on a midway without customers understanding what was being said or even speak in the ring. The tradition is now obsolete.

In the carnival circuit, customers were derisively referred to as "marks," and the term was later adopted by professional wrestling. Marks were deemed easy targets to be separated from their money. Here, two assumed marks don costumes and pose for a photograph behind a backdrop, another big money-maker for carnivals. Hopefully neither was lured into the ring in the nearby tent.

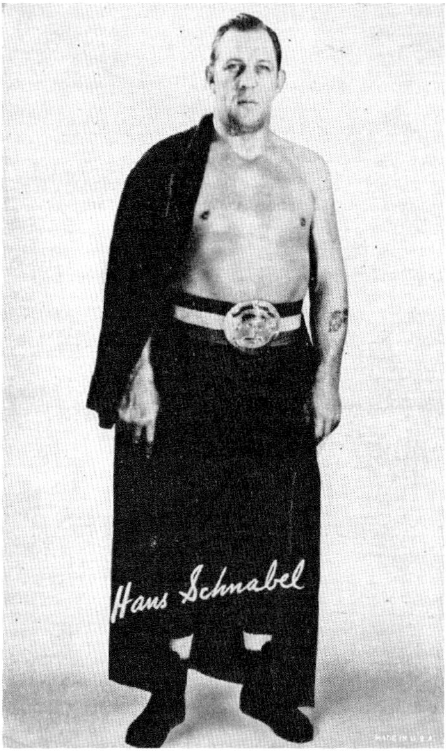

Hans Shabel was the first of the villainous "German" wrestlers, doing his thing even before World War II to the displeasure of the crowd. His unpopularity with the audience was his formula for success, as crowds came hoping to see him defeated. When he won, they would be back the next week, rooting for his demise.

Local Masonic lodge members tended to be big patrons of the Akron matches and with good reason. Over the decades, many of their Masonic brothers—such as Frank Gotch, Wild Red Berry, Dr. Jerry Graham, Whipper Billy Watson, Lord Layton, Rod Fenton, Darren Davenport, the Time Traveler, and famed commentator Gordon Solie—came to the Akron/Cleveland area at different intervals.

Citizens of New Philadelphia gather before a parade and street fair. Such events often included boxing or wrestling shows in tents. One of the most elaborate street fairs came to Canton, between New Philadelphia and Akron in the early 1900s, offering several straight days of wrestling.

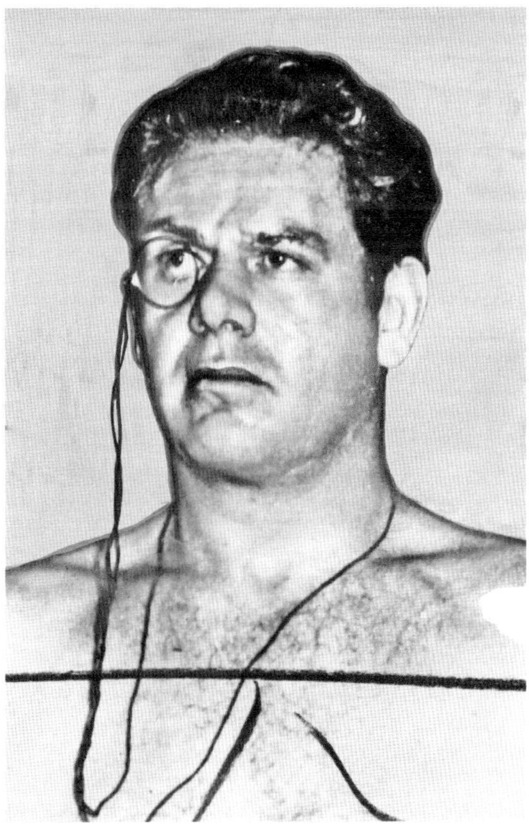

Lord Carlton was another early "ethnic villain" in the game, who toured the United States as an underhanded British nobleman. In real life, he was an accomplished artist away from the ring. His surviving paintings have become both rare and valuable.

Henry Newhouse was an established fan and supporter of Akron wrestling shows before he moved his family to Florida. Every promotion and town saw its regulars, who, in some cases, saw attendance at the matches a life and death matter. A number of these fans may well have known more about wrestling history than the participants.

The East Market Garden (pictured here) and South Main Street Garden held occasional wrestling cards, though their primary function was to serve as dance halls. Don Eagle, the Boatman, and Gil Lacross were some of the wrestlers who appeared during these shows. (Courtesy Summit County Library.)

Construction for the Akron Armory began in downtown Akron in 1916 and was finished in 1918. Seen here, the 3,000-seat arena became a long-standing haven for wrestling, serving Summit County fans for decades. (Courtesy Summit County Library.)

By World War II onward, wrestlers were assuming the roles of heroes and villains with alarming consistency. The wrestling world became a morality play or battleground where good met evil head on. Here, an unidentified villain cheats to win his match at a spot show in the Akron suburbs, just as his predecessors did before him.

An airship hovers over Akron, while below, the trained eye may spot the Akron Armory, Polsky's department store, the St. Bernard Cathedral, the Baltimore & Ohio Railroad (B&O) train station, and more. (Courtesy Crumby Collectibles.)

2

THE ARMORY ERA

The Akron Armory became the focal point for many performing arts and sports in Summit County but most notably for professional wrestling. Things really started to boom

When local businessman Walter Moore took over promotional efforts and began booking new faces through the offices in Chicago, Detroit, Phoenix, Buffalo, and Columbus, the quality of the shows really accelerated. Moore might have gone on forever, had he not won $300,000 in a lottery, after which he decided to retire and move to Florida. He lived quietly there until he died.

Little did Walter Moore know that when he moved away, the historic building would eventually die as well. The stadium fell in disarray, and though others tried to rent the arena to run shows, the administration deemed the place unusable for civic function. The last hurrah came long after the fact when, in 1980, wrestling scenes were shot in the armory for the movie *All the Marbles*.

Everything wrapped up in 1982 when the Akron Armory was torn down. Now only the lonely national guardsman statue holds vigil within a park where the once-glorious building stood.

On your way home, or at any time—

For the BEST in

FINE FOODS • LIQUOR • MIXED DRINKS

Stop at

DEL FESSLER'S BAR

4 E. Exchange St. — BL. 0273

GIL LaCROSSE

WALTER J. MOORE

presents

ALL STAR WRESTLING

EVERY SATURDAY NIGHT

AKRON ARMORY

This is your Lucky Number Programe

Drawing on $25.00 War Bond

8:30 Sharp

No. 531

PRICE 10 Cents

This c. 1943 program from the Akron Armory boasts Gil LaCrosse as a top draw. LaCrosse was a great favorite of the fans, who racked up a long winning streak in Summit County. During the 1940s, this man was one of Ohio's most popular wrestlers, though he never became an international figure.

Roland "Red" Bastien came to Akron in the 1960s for a number of matches at the armory. After retirement, he spent several years as a road agent for the World Wrestling Federation and died in 2012.

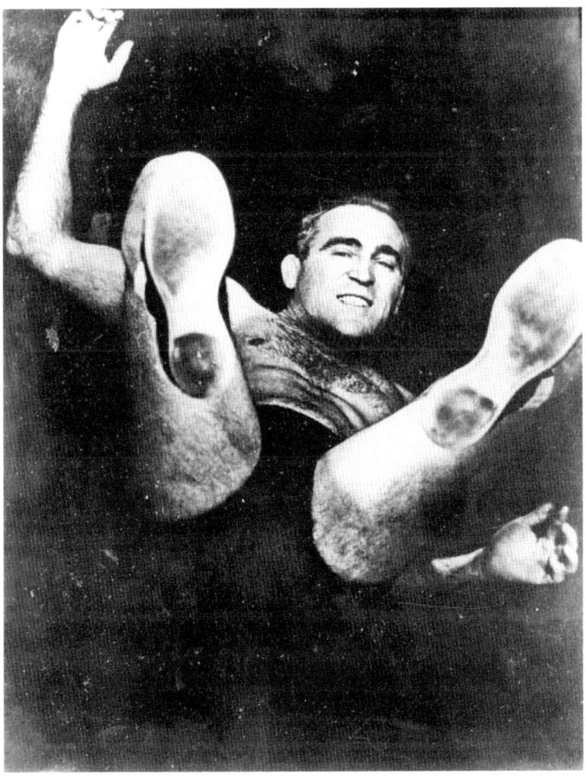

Talented Marvin Mercer dropkicks into the camera in this imposing photograph. Pushed heavily by Columbus promoter Al Haft, Mercer was a regular throughout Ohio in the 1950s and a charismatic fan favorite.

On your way home, or at any time—

For the BEST in

FINE FOODS • LIQUOR • MIXED DRINKS

Stop at

DEL FESSLER'S BAR

4 E. Exchange St. — BL. 0273

THE SWEDISH ANGEL

This is your Lucky Number Programe

Drawing on $25.00 War Bond

8:30 Sharp

N° 094

PRICE 10 Cents

A program carries the name of the Swedish Angel for a 1944 card at the Akron Armory. Angelic wrestlers who were anything but heavenly in style were once a big attraction in wrestling. There was also a French Angel, Polish Angel and Super Swedish Angel at around the same time.

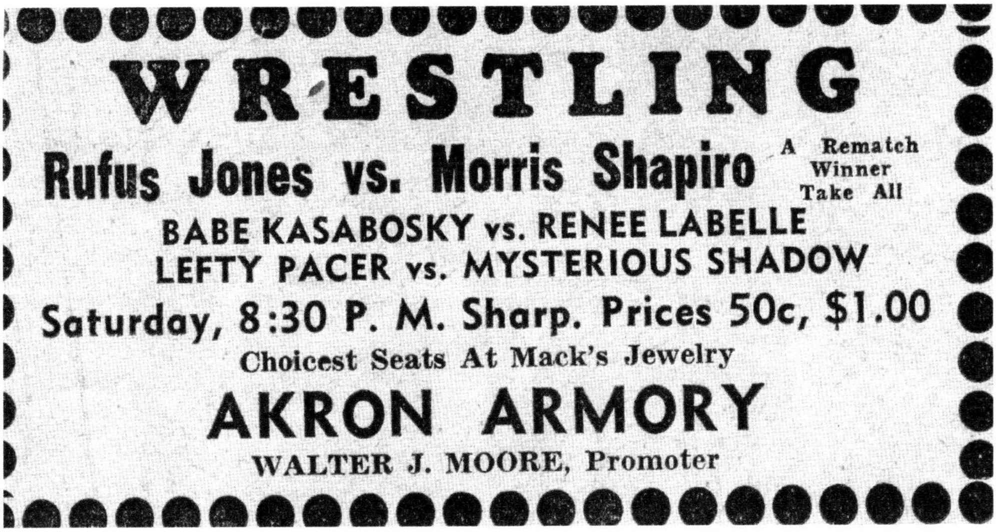

WRESTLING

Rufus Jones vs. Morris Shapiro A Rematch Winner Take All

BABE KASABOSKY vs. RENEE LABELLE

LEFTY PACER vs. MYSTERIOUS SHADOW

Saturday, 8:30 P. M. Sharp. Prices 50c, $1.00

Choicest Seats At Mack's Jewelry

AKRON ARMORY

WALTER J. MOORE, Promoter

This newspaper advertisement for an Akron Armory show highlights the appearance of Morris "Mighty Atlas" Shapiro, who was known for his feats of strength as well as wrestling. Shapiro would often do certain impressive side acts, such as placing an anvil on his stomach and letting someone strike it with a mallet as he tightened his muscles. He showed no ill effect from the blow.

Don Eagle was perhaps one of the most beloved wrestlers to ever appear in Akron, where his father, War Eagle, once worked for Firestone Tire before entering the ring and training his son, seen here locking his famed flying head scissors on a rival, to do the same. The father outlived the son; in a fit of depression, Don committed suicide. (Courtesy Acme Archives/Bob Crumby Collectibles.)

Dave "Legs" Levin, as his nickname suggested, was known for lower rather than upper body strength. He was famous for leg locks, head scissors, and body scissors holds that squeezed men into submission. (Courtesy Jason Sanderson.)

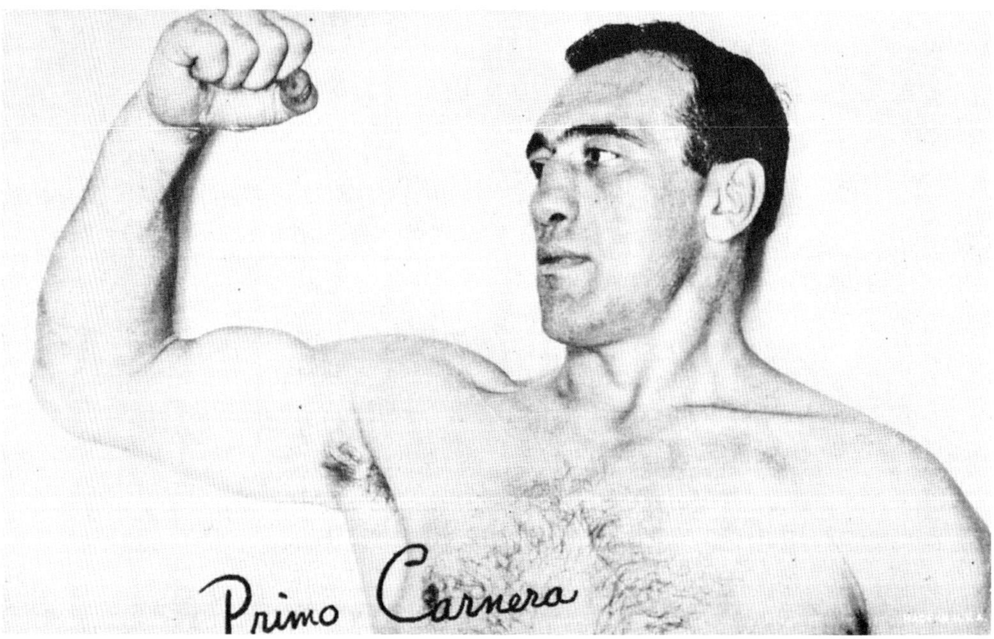

Boxing champion Primo Carnera shifted to wrestling after retirement and became quite established in this field. He worked a full schedule traveling the world but managed some stops in Ohio. He beat Len Montana in 1955 via a disqualification before a very large armory crowd and showed great displeasure in the outcome by chasing the referee out of the ring.

World champion Mildred Burke was one of the most formidable female grapplers of all time. She made appearances in Akron over the years, including one ignoble 1939 encounter where instead of wrestling like normal, she ended up fighting in a pool of mud as part of an uncanny mud wrestling show. (Courtesy Jason Sanderson.)

Seen here is a rare signed index card from Buddy Rogers. "Natureboy" Buddy Rogers was a hated top draw in Akron, long before he won the world title. At the Akron Armory, Rogers wrestled Billy Darnell and Tony Sinatra, among others, and was always jeered. In one odd instance, he found himself cheered when facing hated villain Hans Schmidt in an October 1954 encounter.

Six-time world champion Lou Thesz was as colorless as Buddy Rogers was flamboyant, which made their encounters all the more exciting. A tremendous physical specimen, Thesz lived to be 86 and died in 2002. His cremated ashes were scattered along the banks of the Merrimac River in Missouri. (Courtesy Lanza Archives.)

"IRISH" McGEE

WALTER J. MOORE

presents

ALL STAR WRESTLING

EVERY SATURDAY NIGHT

AKRON ARMORY

This is your Lucky Number Programe

Drawing on $25.00 War Bond

8:30 Sharp

Nº 034 PRICE 10 Cents

This is another Akron program featuring "Irish" McGee, who was a regular in this venue, along with a main event grudge match starring the popular Tex Riley versus Dutch Shultz. Riley would die after a wrestling match in 1964 due to a heart attack in Savannah, Georgia, shortly after he and tag partner Joe Scarpa lost a match to the Von Brauners.

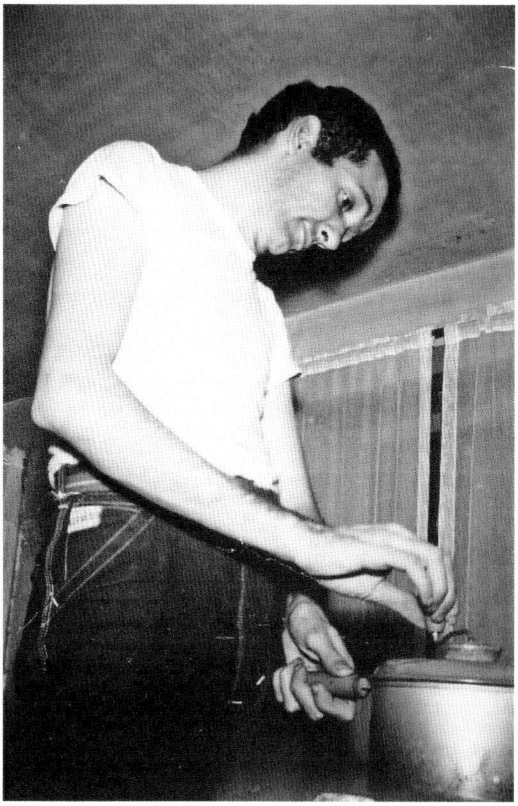

Wrestling fan Joseph Adamov was not always a welcome sight at the armory. He only showed up at ringside when relatives were in town, but his taunts and sometimes drunken insults were so bold, security ordered him to tone things down. One time, Bulldog Brower took things into his own hands and chased Adamov across the arena. Adamov died in 1980 from smoke inhalation in a boardinghouse fire on Market Street.

Bolo Mongol interferes in a match and throws some punches from the ringside floor in true villain form. Beppo, Geeto and Bolo were supposedly Mongolian brothers, but in truth, they were not Mongols or brothers.

Luis Martinez drew some of his largest crowds in the Southwest, where he was good at pulling in the Hispanic crowd as he feuded with Don Kent, Don Arnold, and Killer Brooks, but he was also a mainstay in the Midwest and at the Akron Armory, where he maintained a number of feuds.

Hans Schmidt spent over two decades annoying the Akron fans as a villainous Nazi when he was actually Guy Larose of Canada. This photograph shows him walking from the ring after a win in 1972, as his career was drawing to a close.

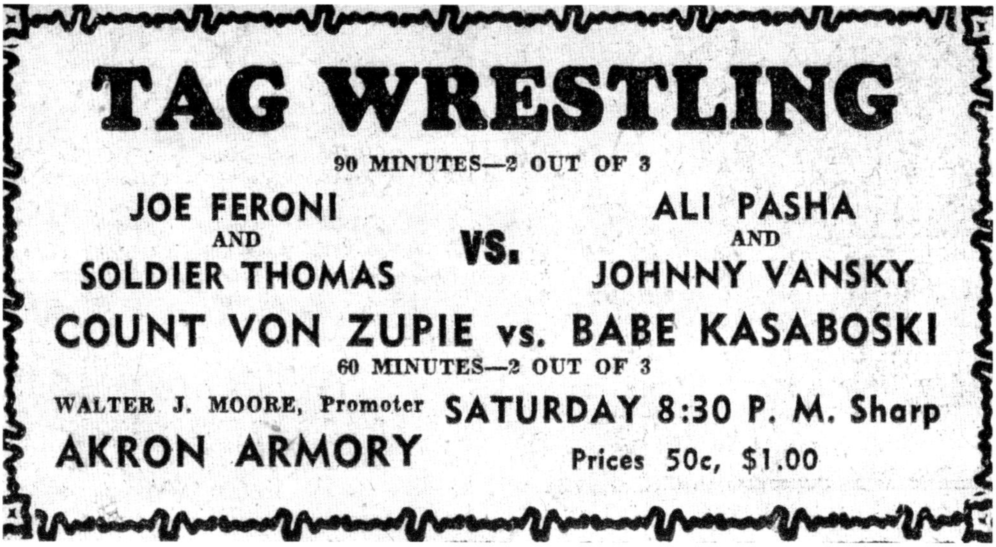
TAG WRESTLING

90 MINUTES—2 OUT OF 3

JOE FERONI AND SOLDIER THOMAS VS. ALI PASHA AND JOHNNY VANSKY

COUNT VON ZUPIE vs. BABE KASABOSKI

60 MINUTES—2 OUT OF 3

WALTER J. MOORE, Promoter SATURDAY 8:30 P. M. Sharp

AKRON ARMORY Prices 50c, $1.00

Shown here is a newspaper clip for an Akron Armory card carrying the name of Ali Pasha. The unfortunate grappler would later die in Pennsylvania via a heart attack following a match. Pasha, like many who chose to wrestle past his prime until his heart gave out, joins the ranks of Jim Wright, Iron Mike, Ray Gunkle, Tex Riley, King Kong Kirk, and Ohio's own Chief Bootnacka, who all passed away from wrestling-related heart attacks around the world.

Don Red Cloud was really Herman Watson, a metal worker in Barberton by day and "Native American" wrestler by night. Due to his welding skills, he also built wrestling rings in his spare time.

On your way home, or at any time—
For the BEST in
FINE FOODS • LIQUOR • MIXED DRINKS
Stop at
DEL FESSLER'S BAR
4 E. Exchange St. — BL. 0273

MAE WESTON
The Louisiana Wildcat
Meets the winner of to-
night's match, next Satur-
day night.

This is your Lucky Number Programe
Drawing on $25.00 War Bond
8:30 Sharp
No. 235
PRICE 10 Cents

Pictured is another Akron program featuring the addition of woman wrestlers Mae Young and Elvira Snodgrass, the latter of whom wrestled as a barefoot hillbilly and was extremely popular with the fans. Other women who appeared in the armory over the years included Heather Feather, Sue Green, Sandy Parker, Paula Kaye, Kay Casey, Babs Wingo, Linda Klein, and Mae Weston. Weston, pictured on this program, was set to take on the winner of the Young-Snodgrass match.

Though the armory was the key place for Akron area wrestling, occasional spot shows, like the one pictured here, took place in the suburbs, usually as charity events for high schools. The spot shows or matches, held off the regular circuit of towns, were sometimes lavish events. At other times they were subpar cards, depending on the promoter, roster, and budget.

Dave McKigney of Canada was a regular in Ohio and also seen on Akron television with decent reception in the old WWF television show that came from Pittsburgh. He was better known for growing long hair and a beard later on to become the Wild Bearman.

The People's Savings & Trust Company Of Akron ran occasional ads of this type in the Akron Armory programs, as did Jimandy's Drive Inn Restaurant, the Federal Cigar Store, Diana Grill, Luse Display Company, and other sponsors.

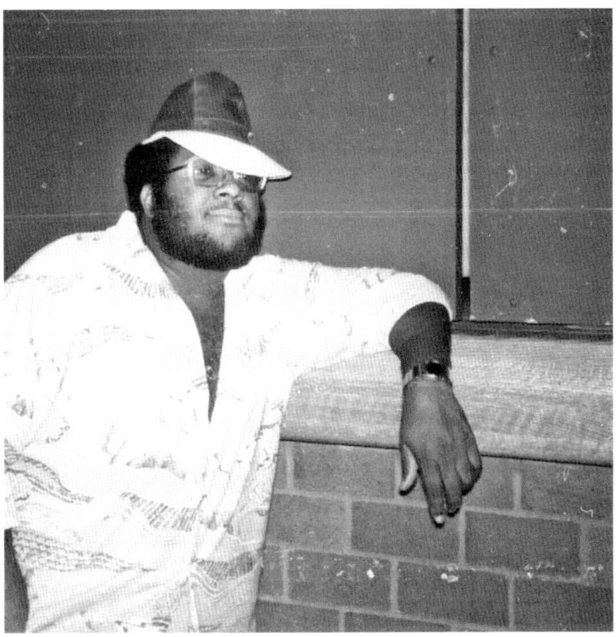

Jimmie Banks of Akron was a popular wrestler who died way too young from kidney failure a few years after the armory closed. His funeral was attended by a number of prominent area wrestlers, including Zoltan, the North American Madman, the Hogg Brothers, and Mad Dog Marcial Bovee. A big memorial card after his death, with wrestlers working for free and funds going to the family, also proved to be a financial success.

From the 1950s into the 1970s, the Sheik remained one of the all-time top draws in Akron. He had bloody matches with Bobo Brazil, Johnny Powers, and Tony Marino in this venue, but he was by no means restricted to Akron. The Sheik worked a constant circuit in the Ohio-Michigan area, which stood to reason, as he was a longtime behind-the-scenes Detroit promoter and a matchmaking powerhouse.

At the height of his drawing prowess in Akron, the Sheik tried to take his feuds to Arizona and expand his promotion, but the overhead was too great, and he lasted only six months. This match shows him facing rival Dory Funk Jr. in Phoenix.

Dory Funk Jr. staggers from the ring with a deep gash from the Sheik's ever-present pencil, hidden in his boot and pulled out undetected to the referee at the time. Though the Phoenix venture failed, Sheik and Funk were back expanding their feud throughout Ohio in short order.

Following World War II and into the 1970s, old hatred was played upon with a host of Nazi villains such as Fritz Von Goring, Hans Schmidt, and Kurt Von Hess, pictured here. Whether as a single act or with his tag team partner Karl Von Shotz, Von Hess was a master villain; though in truth, he was an easy going Canadian from the Hamilton area. (Courtesy Paige Von Hess Sutherland.)

Another of the great ethnic villains was Tor Kamata, who looked and sounded like something off a World War II propaganda poster. In reality, he was a Hawaiian named Macronald Kamaka, and his name was a twist on Spanish Inquisitor Tomas Torquemada to sound sinister.

Tony Vallota, a well-known photographer out of Pennsylvania, started taking pictures at matches as a teen and continues to do so to this day, decades later. He made several trips to the Akron Armory, where he was a familiar face.

Johnny Powers of Canada was a main-eventer in Akron, Cleveland, and Canton, though he looks a bit worse for wear while on the receiving end of some punishment from an unnamed opponent at a spot show.

In spite of his apparent suffering here, Powers came back to win this match, as he usually did. Throughout Ohio, he was better known for his feuds with Bulldog Brower, Eric the Red, and the Sheik.

Powers used two finishing holds to end most of his matches: his Powers Leap off the top rope, as demonstrated here, and his Powers Lock, a figure-four leg lock that few people ever escaped from.

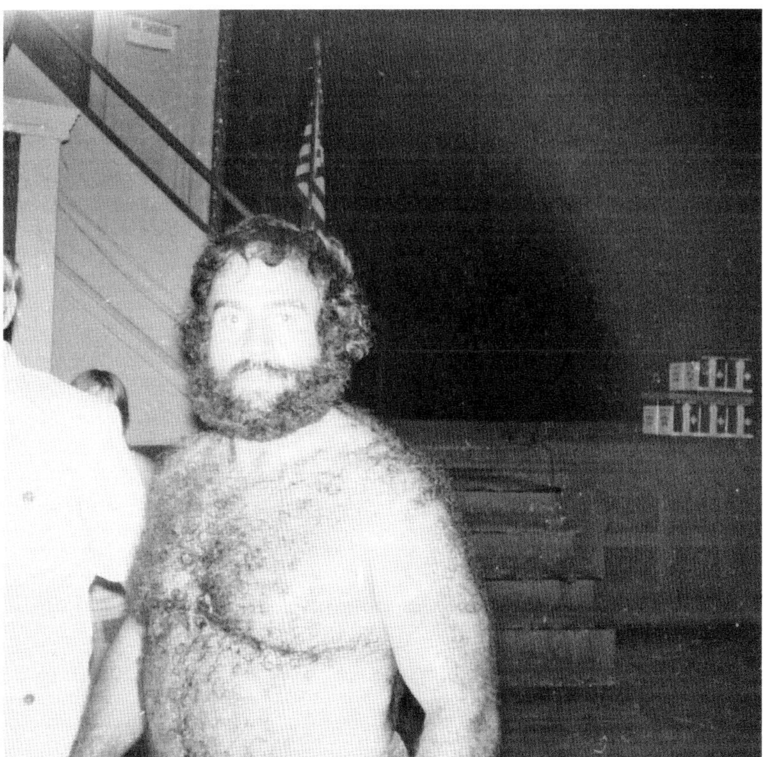

The Sicilian Beast looked like a villain, but he was a favorite of Akron fans, though he did use a bawling style. He is seen here in a 1974 armory pose before facing one of the Mongols.

The interior of the Akron Armory and the majestic glass window becomes visible behind Bolo Mongol, who awaits his challenger in the ring. Surprisingly, no wrestler ever fell through the window to his death on the street below.

Juan Rebbaca heads back to the locker room, looking the worst for wear after a bout with Gil Guerrero in the early 1970s. Rebbaca and Guerrero has a long-lasting feud that spanned Ohio and Indiana in the early 1970s, with Guerrero winning most of the confrontations.

Abdullah the Butcher was perhaps the Sheik's greatest rival when it came to outright villainousness. Billed as an insane wildman from Sudan, he was actually one Larry Shreve from Canada. (Courtesy Bob Crumby Collectables.)

Sky Low Low was a famed midget wrestler deriving his ring name as the antithesis of gigantic Texas grappler Sky Hi Lee. His real name was Marcel Gauntier, and he came from Canada, though the bulk of his career was spent in the United States. He died in 1998. (Courtesy Tony Lanza archives.)

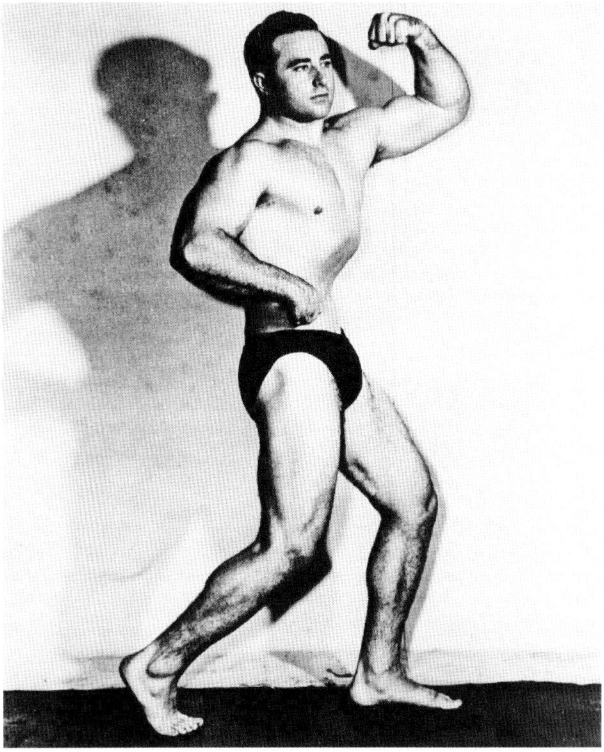

"Professor" Roy Shire often wore a graduation gown and cap into the ring as he stressed both physical and intellectual superiority over all those around him. He eventually retired from the ring and started promoting his own shows in the Las Vegas–San Francisco area. (Courtesy Jason Sanderson.)

At six feet, six inches and 300 pounds, radio and television personality Malcolm "Big" Wilson was large enough to wrestle but never did, though he was acquainted with many Akron- and Cleveland-area wrestlers and other celebrities. After a long stint in Ohio, he moved southward to Florida and died in Selma, Alabama, while on a promotional tour in 1989.

Pittsburgh-native Johnny De Fazio made appearances at the Akron Armory, as well as at many other stops in the Ohio-Pennsylvania area. Upon retirement, he entered the realm of politics. During his prime, De Fazio was recognized for a vast knowledge of holds and sensational flying dropkicks.

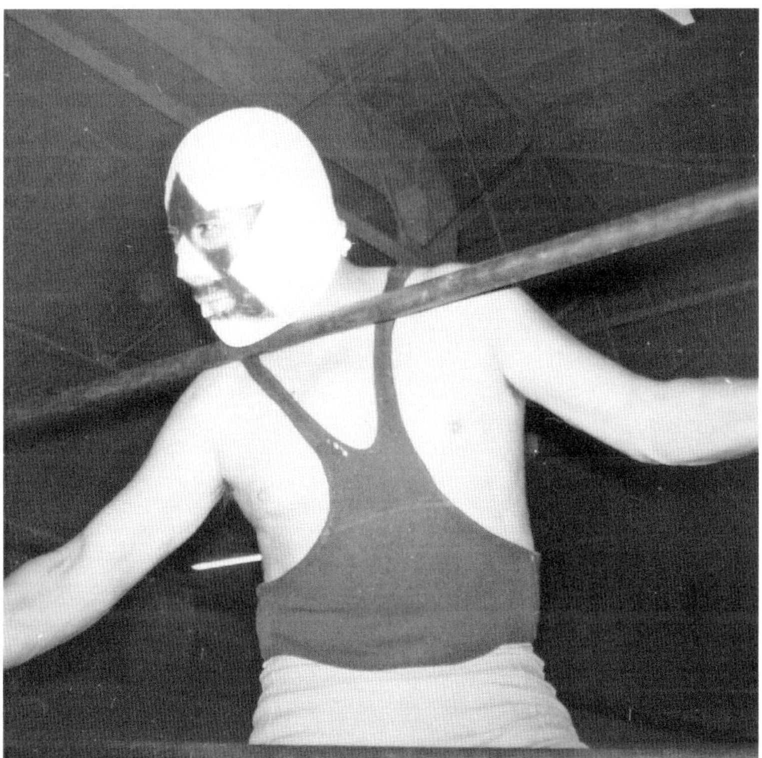

The Patriot, complete with a star on his mask, struts his stuff before the Akron crowd. Though he had a colorful routine, he was never a regular on armory cards.

Hank James smirks as he heads toward the ring for a 1974 match, exemplifying arrogance in motion. After a feud with the Sheik, however, James went from villain to fan favorite.

Taking long walks to the ring infuriated the fans, as seen here in a sequence of photographs with Hank James still strutting down the aisle. James was a master at using little tricks like the slow walk or a mere smirk to ignite the audience against him, which, as a wrestling villain, was his job.

Akron fans also frequented the Cleveland Sports Arena on Euclid Avenue in downtown Cleveland, which featured many of the same wrestlers as seen at the Akron Armory. Sadly, the building shared the same fate as the armory and was likewise torn down. (Courtesy Cleveland Public Library.)

Mil Mascaras was an international draw and one of the biggest stars to come out of Mexico. His schedule was hectic, but he did make Ohio appearances on a limited basis. Aside from wrestling, Mascaras was also a major movie star in his native land, with a number of films to his credit, playing himself as a super hero under his huge assortment of masks.

The feud between Dominic Denucci and Don Kent spilled from Akron to all parts of Ohio, as exhibited in this Canton encounter. More often than not, their encounters ended in bloody double disqualifications with neither man coming out the victor.

Cheating to gain an advantage as usual, Don Kent pulls a chain from his trunks and prepares to use it on Dominic Denucci. The referee misses seeing the illegal object, but everyone else in the arena notices.

Bloody Don Kent stumbles from the ring after his wild Canton encounter with Dominic Denucci, with the full knowledge that rematches will take place again and again as part of their traveling feud. Though Kent was a brawler who prided himself on making the other man bleed, he did receive doses of his own medicine at Denucci's hands and ended up bloody himself.

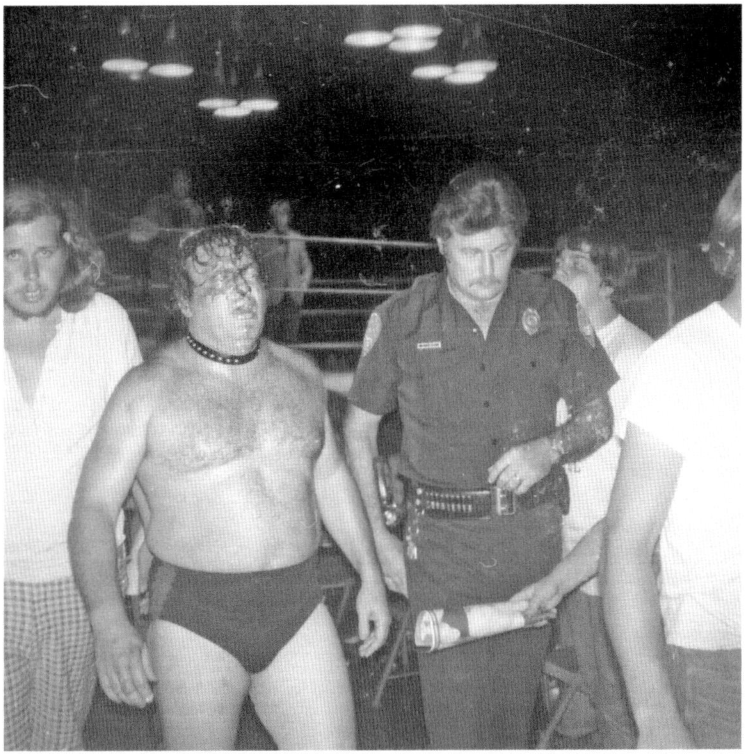

Dominic Denucci likewise heads for the locker room, knowing he and Kent will meet in much-hyped rematches throughout Ohio. Though Denucci feuded regularly with Kent, he also found time for many wild matches with the Fabulous Fargo brothers, the Sheik, and Abdullah the Butcher.

Kurt Von Hess stomps toward the ring where Aztec Joe awaits, while the boos of the crowd ring in his ears. The standard Nazi villain was always a guaranteed draw in Akron, where patriotic Americans came to shout for the good old hometown boys to beat anyone they were matched against.

Bobo Brazil of Benton Harbor, Michigan, was one of the first great African American wrestlers in the profession and a worldwide star. He had many matches in Akron, including face-offs with his key rival, the Sheik.

The Crusader was a popular wrestler in Akron, who was actually Canadian star Dewey Robertson under a mask. Though always a man in terrific physical condition, he eventually faced prostate cancer after retirement, a final battle he was unable to win.

Here, the Crusader taunts his opponent, Hank James, to enter the ring and do battle. James, as usual, spent several minutes outside the ring, stalling and jawing with the crowd to build "heat," or fan reaction, for the match.

Pictured here is an autographed index card from Andre the Giant, who made an Akron Armory appearance in 1974 to face Bulldog Brower. A world-famous star, Andre died in 1993 due to health issues related to his massive size.

The Dark Destroyer looks menacing enough in this posed publicity photograph; however, he was afforded only one match at the Akron Armory, where he faced Bill Bethune in an opening event in the early 1970s.

Another villain was the Mummy, and though he looked like a monster rather than a man, he was actually Benjamin Ramirez. In 1995, the frightening grappler died a horrendous death in a commercial airline accident when an Avianca jet crashed in South America. He had boarded the flight for a vacation to visit relatives.

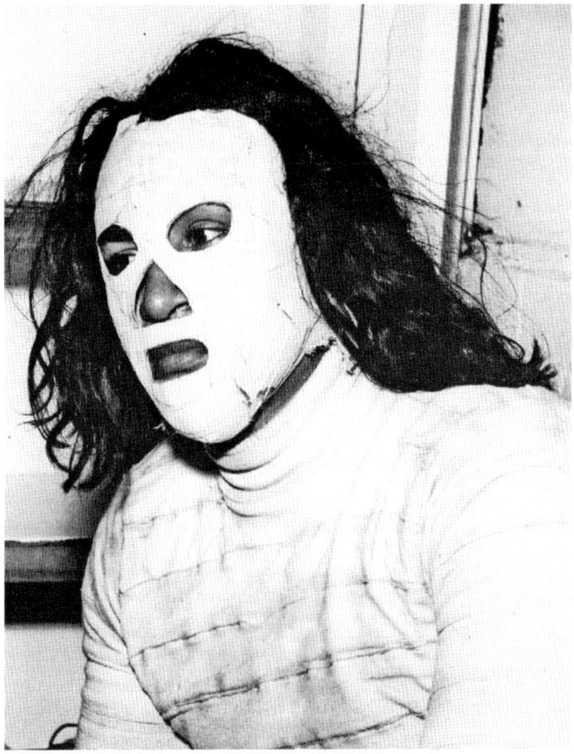

Two-time world champion Whipper Billy Watson was a smiling fan favorite throughout Ohio. He was left a partial invalid after being hit by a car as he crossed the street following retirement and died from a heart attack some years later.

The Mongols discuss their strategy en route to the ring for a 1974 tag team match with the Crusader and the Sicilian Beast. Aside from their Ohio run, the Mongols also proved to be a big draw further east in New York's Madison Square Garden and other major arenas.

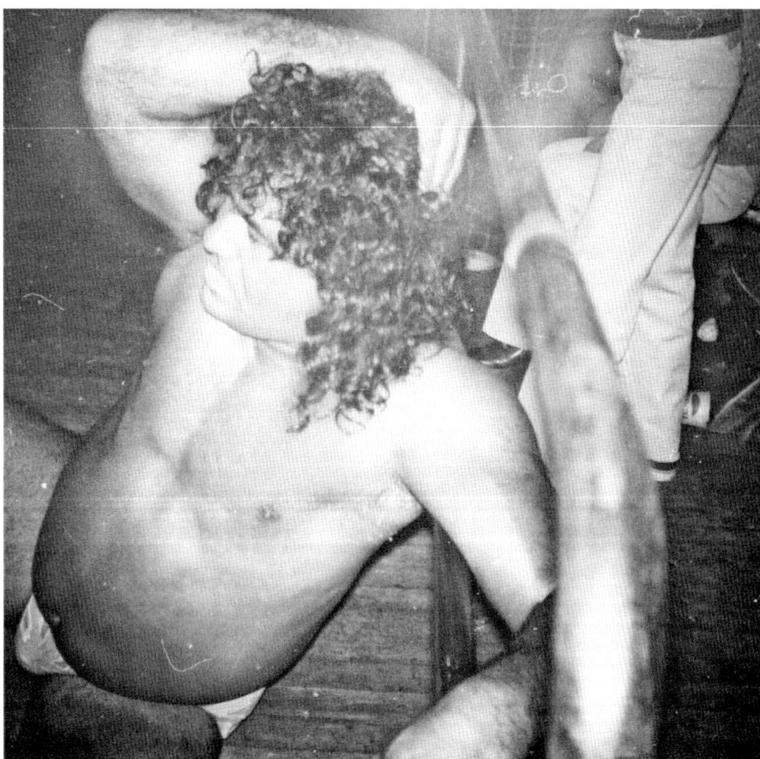

Aztec Joe tries to rally after being tossed from the ring and into the railing by Bull Curry. Though originally Joe's friend, Curry turned on him and attacked him in front of an infuriated armory audience, proving himself the untrustworthy villain he was reputed to be.

Pictured from left to right, Pete McKay, Zoltan the Great, and photographer Tony Vallota discuss an upcoming Akron event at a spot show in Steubenville, Ohio. The river towns were a frequent merging place for wrestlers from both the Akron and Pittsburgh area. The three pictured here are part of the Pennsylvania crew.

Fred Curry rallies while resting on the railing as he prepares to make a comeback in a 1974 armory match. While Fred's father "Bull" usually fought as a bad guy, Fred was a popular fan favorite.

Smiling Greg Watson of Akron was charismatic enough but considered too small to truly make the big time. What he lacked in size and strength, he made up for with sensational aerial moves. He was known for flying dropkicks and elbow smashes.

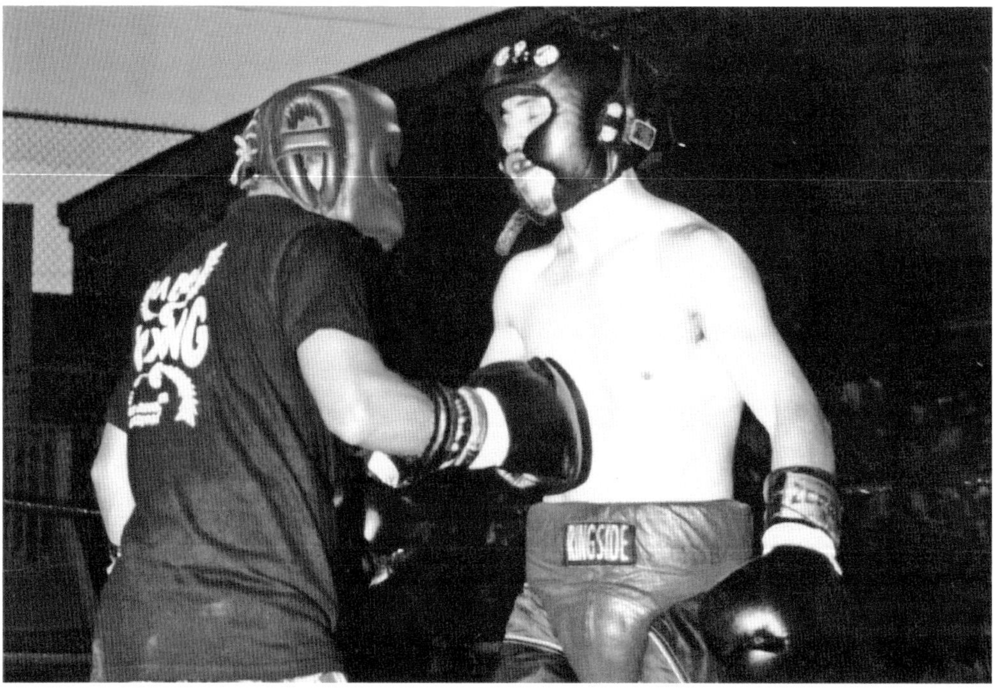

Amateur boxers spar in an Akron gym. Aside from wrestling, Gulden Gloves and professional boxing were big draws in the armory, along with the Shrine Circus, concerts (such as Buddy Holly, Chubby Checker, and Fats Domino), political rallies (for Nixon, Kennedy, and Truman), and business seminars. (Courtesy Ed Ahrens.)

Bull Curry stomps from the ring while glowering at the jeering fans. Some people, however, liked the villains. Note one fearless child stretching out to try to pat Curry on the shoulder.

Killer Brooks heads for the ring one more time in Akron as he readies himself to meet Ben Justice in 1972. He would later convince Justice to turn on friends and fans and team with him as a fellow rule-breaker.

Guy "Stomper" Mitchell smiles before a match in 1974. He would add dye to his hair and become Jerry Valient, joining brothers Jimmy and Johnny in the 1980s. He finally retired to Indiana after a career spanning decades and passed away in 2011.

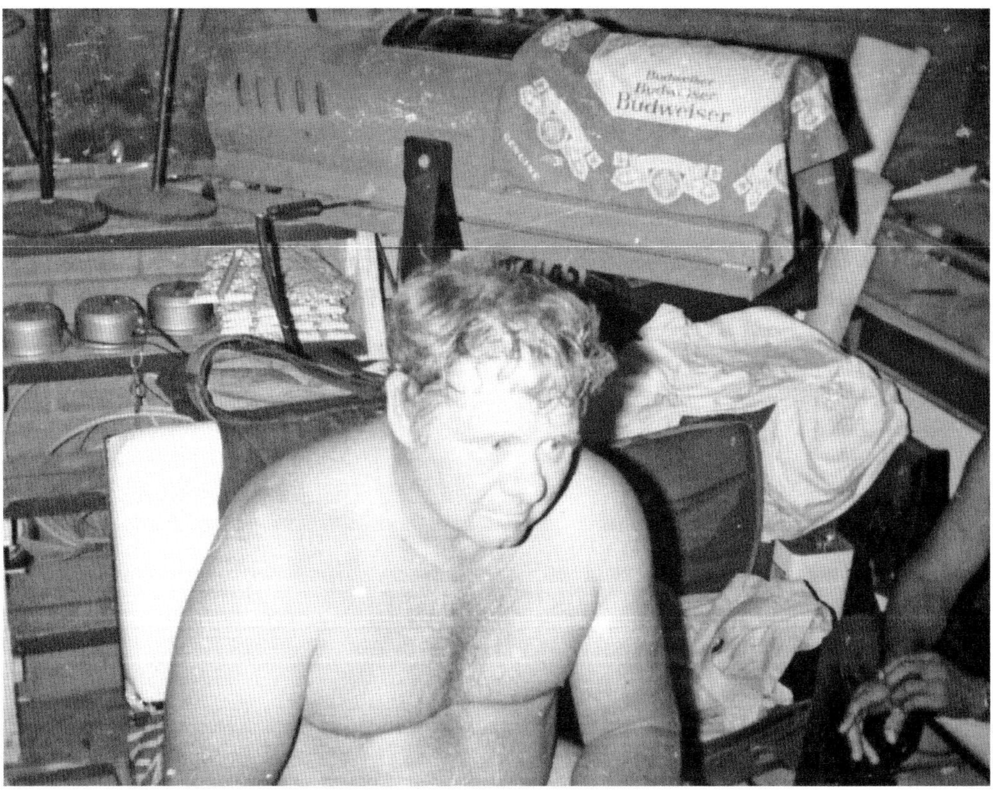

In the early 1970s, several wrestlers from the Tennessee circuit came to the armory briefly, including the Von Brauners, Lanny Poffo, Gentleman Saul, and Pez Whately. Rip Tyler, seen here, wanted to appear in Akron but could not agree on a suitable payment, so he stayed in Nashville.

Manager Bad Boy Hines shows his displeasure over a decision by attacking the referee. Hines was never an Ohio regular and generally came into the area as a package deal with promoters. He and several Tennessee wrestlers would carpool together.

The author poses with Charles "Easy Coast Charlie" Yoder, one of wrestling's many fanatical supporters. He was a patron of armory shows from the 1940s up to its closing and an attendee at other shows elsewhere in Akron until his death. Yoder also wrote for some wrestling newsletters, called fan sheets, in his last years.

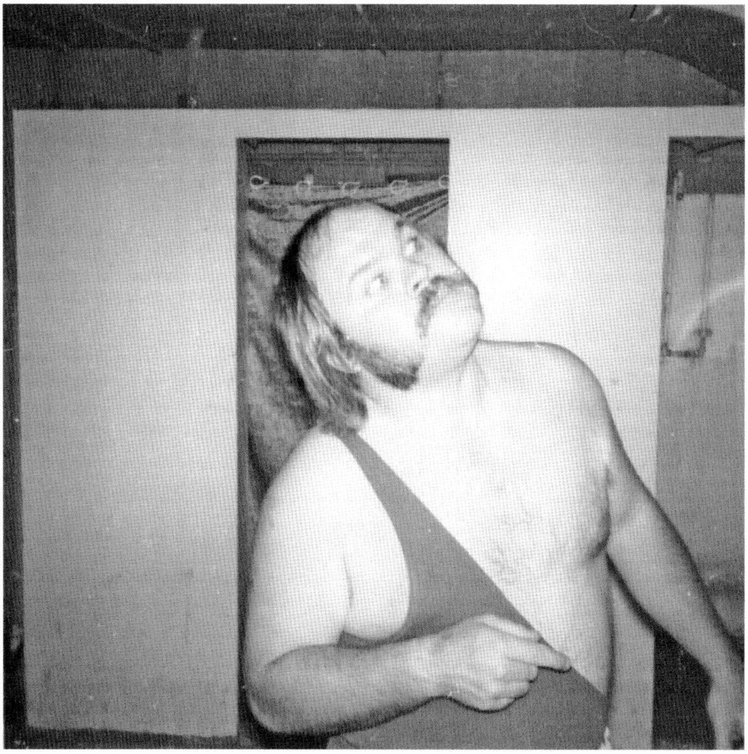

"Maniac" Mike Gordon of Springfield appeared on varied Akron television shows, but like some of his associates, he was never booked for a house show in the armory. He eventually moved to Phoenix, where he became a main-eventer in the 1970s. He retired in 1985, moved to Canada, married a Canadian woman, and died from a heart attack in 2010.

Ben Justice was a fan favorite billed from Washington, DC, who worked the Ohio circuit for years, first as a "good guy" and then as a villain. Justice was most famous for his sleeper hold, in which he put opponents out with this move, cutting off the blood flow to the brain.

Dominic Denucci smiles for a close-up photograph prior to a match with Kabooki at the armory. Denucci was always a beloved figure in Akron, but he was especially popular with the Italian-American patrons who continually came to cheer him on.

Mike Loren originally wrestled as Porky the Pig and brought a live pig to the ring with him. He later tried to get away from the "Porky" moniker and go as Iron Mike, but the fans would never let him forget his original alias.

Mike Mazurki shifted between wrestling and acting, with many contending his roles on film and television far surpassed any of his antics in the ring. Movies to his credit include *Damnation Alley, Some Like it Hot, Challenge to be Free, Mob Boss,* and *Murder, My Sweet*, and he was seen in episodes of *Gunsmoke, Gilligan's Island, Fantasy Island,* and *Charlie's Angels* on the small screen.

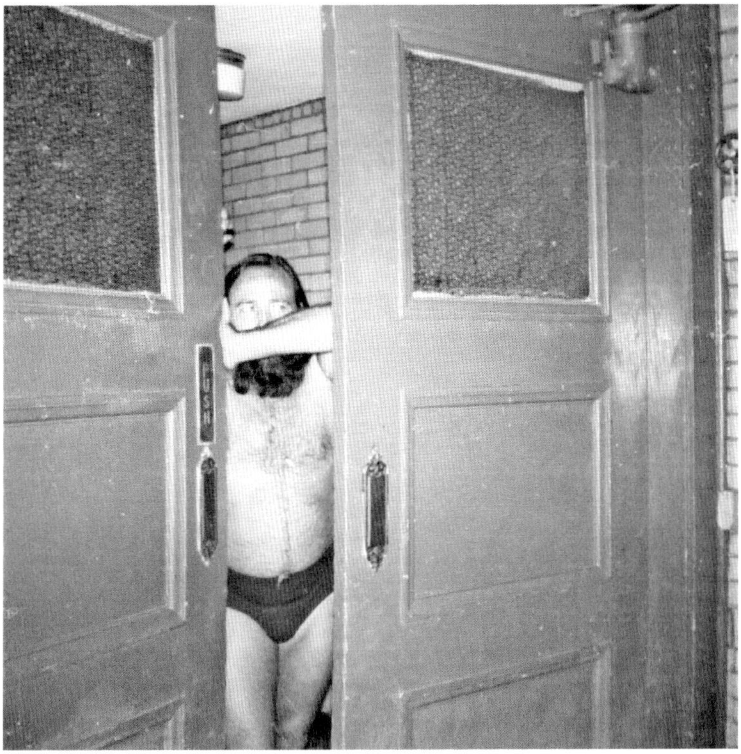

Killer Brooks watches the action from the dressing room door. A few seconds later, a young fan approached him to ask for an autograph, and in true villain form, Brooks slammed the door in his face.

The Akron wrestling crew and some diehard fans also made trips to towns on the Ohio River for spot shows, such as Steubenville, East Liverpool, Bridgeport, Mingo Junction, Toronto, and Marietta, as well as across the border in West Virginia. Most of these shows were routine, barring one in 1951 in East Liverpool, where 19-year-old Jeanie Wolf died from injuries received in a tag team match.

Veteran wrestler, boxer, trainer, and promoter Paavo Katonan of Arizona never had a permanent trade agreement with Walter Moore but was instrumental in getting several Arizona-area wrestlers booked in Akron, such as Monte Ladue, Rod Fenton and Don Arnold.

Though photographed by someone in the back seat, the distinct form of a member of the ring crew is visible from behind as he drives into Akron for a show during a rainstorm. The ring crew was a vital part of each show, as one ring was set up, taken down, and moved from location to location.

Most wrestlers appearing in Akron worked a circuit where they drove or took a train, but an occasional major star or champion making a "spot appearance" had to be flown in. Usually, such stars would arrive at the Akron Municipal Airport south of town. The airport was eventually closed and turned into a restaurant.

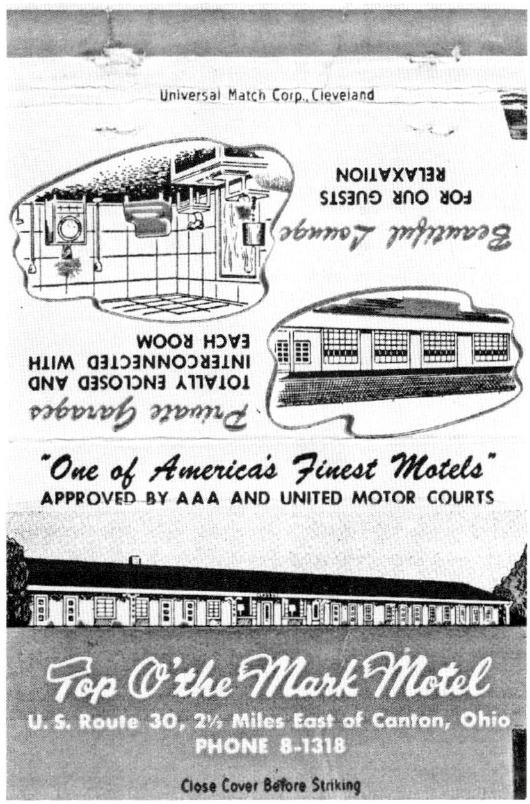

This is a matchbook from a popular motel in Canton. Though there was lodging closer to the armory, many wrestlers, being a penny-pinching lot, preferred this location for economic reasons. One of the tricks wrestlers would pull would be for a single person to book the room, then a whole carload of other wrestlers would sneak in and sleep on the floor to save money.

Pictured here is a fancier program from the early 1970s. Names like Buddy Rogers, Primo Carnera, and Ali Pasha were replaced by the likes of Waldo Von Eric, Tex McKenzie, and Abdullah the Butcher, but the action was still fast and furious.

Ronnie Lee of Akron was a beloved local hero before knee injuries put him out of wrestling, causing him to retire and move to Florida. When he was not wrestling, he often found added work as a referee.

Shown here is a matchbook for Jimandy's Drive Inn Restaurant in neighboring Cuyahoga Falls. The restaurant was a popular gathering place for both fans and wrestlers, as well as an occasional sponsor of raffle prizes for Walter Moore's promotional efforts.

Dale G. Pierce, the author's father, proudly displays a large box of Snyder Potato Chips won at an Akron Armory wrestling show, when numbers were drawn for prizes at intermission. Such raffles were always popular at the shows, with items varying as Walter Moore's office deemed fit.

Shown here is an autographed index card carrying the signature of "Cowboy" Bob Ellis, a real-life wrestling cowboy who bred racehorses on his ranch. Though cheered by the fans, Ellis was known for an extremely aggressive style which often saw him and his opponent both covered in blood. A star of international fame, Ellis was more popular in neighboring Indiana than Ohio, though he did make occasional appearances in Akron at the armory.

Fred Curry is pictured here in yet another Akron encounter, this time with archrival Killer Brooks. After being tossed from the ring, the popular star rallied for a comeback while the crowd cheered him on. Brooks and Curry met in several brutal encounters, not just in Akron but throughout the Midwest.

Killer Brooks takes a break from the ring during his match with Curry in what was a seesaw bout with the advantage going back and forth between them. The match ended in a bizarre double pin after they collided in mid-ring and fell backward upon each other.

Having all he could take of Fred Curry, Killer Brooks heads for the hills, or more fittingly, the safety of the locker room.

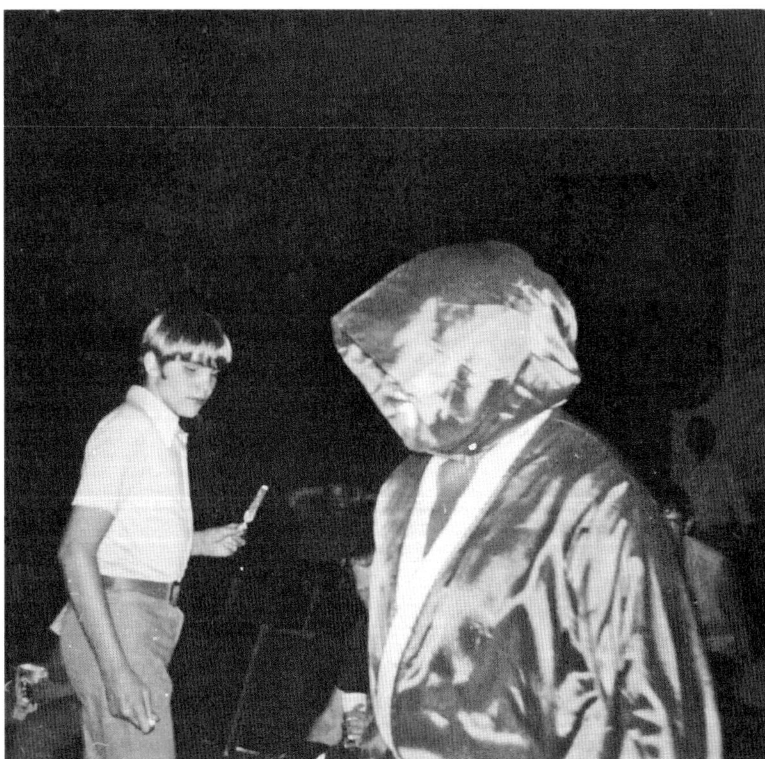

His face hidden with a hood, the Great Kabooki heads toward the ring for an encounter with Dominic Denucci. Kabooki was known for using a handful of salt pulled from a concealed place on his body, which he would rub in the eyes of opponents to win his matches.

Paul "Hell's Angel No. 1" Dupree (real name Charles Harris) sags on the ropes as blood drips from wounds on his head. The Hell's Angels were a detested tag team who appeared regularly at the Akron Armory, as well as other cards in Dayton, Columbus, Springfield, and Toledo.

The referee watches Hell's Angel No. 1 try to revive Ron "Hell's Angel No. 2" Dupree (real name Russell Grobes) as the latter gasps to catch his breath.

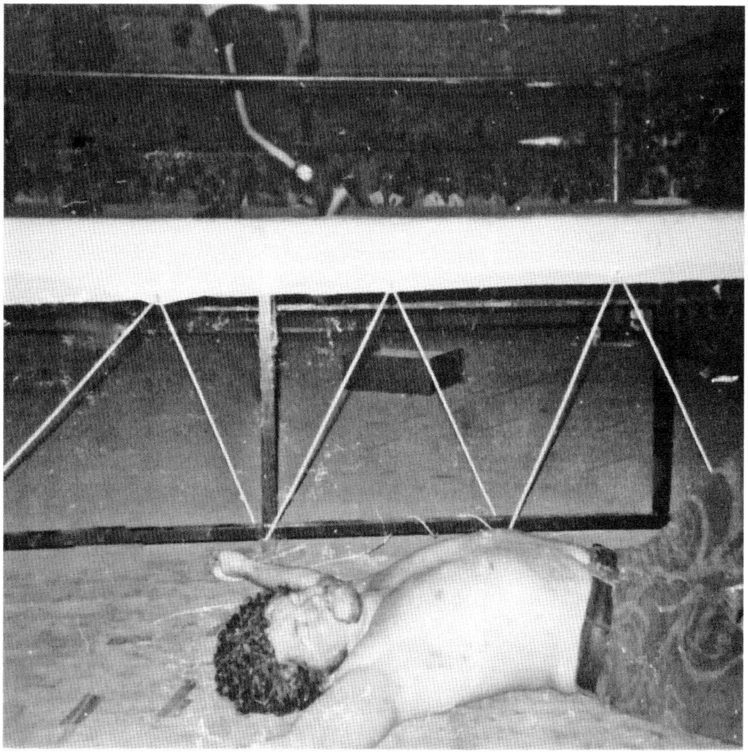

Hell's Angel No. 2 lies outside the ring in the heat of the action at an Ohio spot show. Forced out of active wrestling due to a heart condition, he would become an announcer and die while announcing matches in the ring in Tacoma, Washington, on October 17, 1973.

Shown here is another photograph of Hell's Angel Paul Dupree at a moment of difficulty in an Arizona match, taking a break from the Ohio snow. While Dupree was a regular and main-eventer in the Midwest, he reportedly hated the snow and would try to spend his winters performing in Arizona, Oregon, or Washington.

Chris Markoff claimed to be from Macedonia, Serbia, Russia, and several other locations in a long career. Though he was on the Akron circuit, he went with Macedonia to appeal to the Serbian, Croatian, and Bosnian immigrants and their bloodline in the area.

Originally a villain, Pampero Firpo became a fan favorite when he feuded with the Sheik. He eventually retired from wrestling, moved to California, and took a job with the post office.

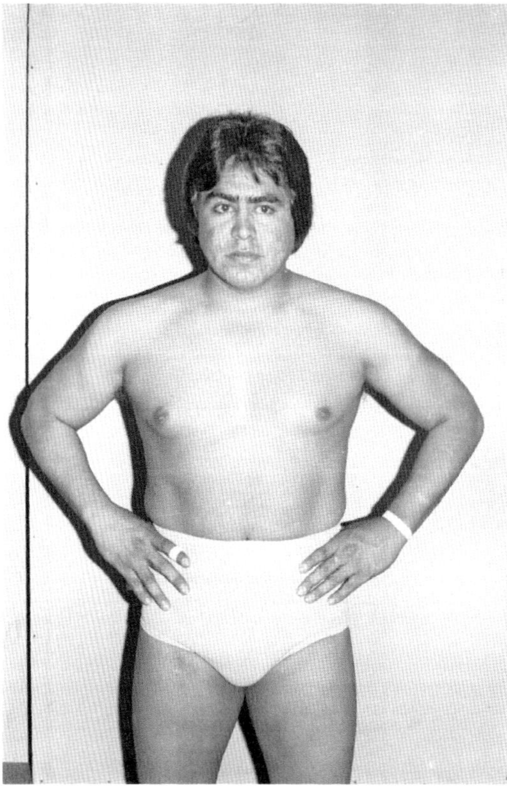

Many wrestlers from the Ohio circuit who headed westward to escape the brutal winters tried to get Benny Mendeblis of Tucson, Arizona, booked into the Akron circuit, but the matchmakers deemed him too small and nixed him from the start. Thus, he remained in Arizona for a long career.

Ventura V. Mendibles
March 31, 1949
April 30, 2012

God saw he was getting tired and the cure was not to be. So He put his arms around him and whispered "Come with me". With tearful hearts we watched him fade away. Although we loved him dearly, we could not make him stay. A golden heart stopped beating; hard working hands to rest, God broke our hearts to prove to us, He only takes the best.

Martinez Funeral Chapels

This is a funeral card for Benny Mendeblis, listing his real name as Ventura Mendeblis, after he passed away from cancer in 2012 without ever making it eastward to wrestle as he had hoped. Instead of heading east, he remained in the west, where he faced a number of visiting wrestlers from Ohio and Michigan.

Pictured from left to right, wrestling announcer Ron Lindsey poses with Dr. Jerry Graham and booking agent Ed Ahrens. Graham was a regular in Ohio from the 1950s through the 1970s, until multiple arrests and no shows caused him to be duly blacklisted. He moved to California and continued to wrestle, but he constantly caused problems behind the scenes there as well. (Courtesy Ed Ahrens.)

Another shot shows Dr. Jerry Graham glowering at the camera with a cigar in his mouth, possibly displaying the effects of too much alcohol during one of his many post-match benders. (Courtesy Ed Ahrens.)

After splitting with "brother" Ron Dupree, Paul Dupree abandoned the Hell's Angels routine in favor of coming from "the future" as Chris Colt and teaming with Count Drummer, who claimed to come from "the past" as the Time Machine. Colt made his last Akron Armory appearances as a single act, losing to John-Boy Ruffin and Rip Hawk in 1976. He is seen here posing with a young fan.

Victor the Wrestling Bear makes a special appearance in Chicago at a Bulls game. In his heyday, Victor toured the United States on a schedule to rival that of any human wrestler. The bear enjoyed a fan base larger than many human counterparts.

Tuffy Truesdale mugs it up with Victor. Aside from being a competent animal trainer, Truesdale was a capable wrestler in his own right with many matches to his credit. He beat an alligator in the armory as noted earlier and also brought Victor to cards in the 1960s.

The end of an era. The Great Kabooki (left) discusses past deeds with fellow retired wrestler Frankie Cain at a 1995 old-timer gathering. Kabooki, as a villain, along with Cain, who became the Great Mephisto, had a lot to talk about. (Courtesy Mike Lano.)

3

After the Armory

Wrestling continued after the closing of the Akron Armory as varied groups vied for the territory. In the 1980s, there was a particularly nasty promotional war between the World Wrestling Federation and the National Wrestling Alliance/World Championship Wrestling at the Breakaway Nightclub in Akron. The former won out, only to abandon Akron in favor of Cleveland, spelling an end to big-time monthly shows.

After Walter Moore packed up shop, many fans headed to other areas for wrestling shows, such as the War Memorial Auditorium, now called the Civic Center in Canton, and the Field House across the border in Erie, Pennsylvania, which continued to feature many of the stars who used to headline at the armory.

In recent years, several promotions have come and gone, while others survive to this day. Though not part of the major offices seen on cable television, the action tends to be fast and furious. Some of the venues that have housed wrestling in one form or another in modern times have included the Shamrock Bar in Barberton and the Knights of Columbus Hall off Waterloo Road in Akron itself, as well as spot shows in a number of dance halls, roller-skating rinks, and gymnasiums.

In 1981, Bruno Sammartino (pictured), Dominic Denucci, Baron Scicluna, Johnny Valient, and others broke with the World Wrestling Federation to form their own show. Booking towns in Pennsylvania and Ohio, they also ran Akron at the Rubber Workers Union Hall. Other wrestlers on their cards included Zoltan the Great, Brady Howard, Jimmie Banks, Hans Mueller, Marcial Bovee, Hans Schroeder, and Ronnie Lee. The group eventually folded, and many of the instigators went back to their former employer.

Louis Mucciolo was primarily known for action out west before traveling eastward where he was Louie Spicolli in the World Championship Wrestling group and Rad Radford in the World Wrestling Federation. For a time, he saw some action in the Midwestern states but was let go and returned westward.

Another posed shot of the unfortunate Louie Spicolli, who would pass away in his apartment in 1998. In death, he became more popular with the fans than he was in real life, becoming somewhat of a James Dean–type figure to many.

Tony Altimore was well known for his years as a tag team partner to Lou Albano as one half of the Sicilians. After both retired, Albano became famous as a manager, and Tony Altimore took the role of a road agent for the WWF, where he was still a familiar face to Ohio and Pennsylvania fans.

The Field House in Erie, Pennsylvania, became a new location for disgruntled Akron fans to see wrestling in the 1970s after the armory ceased to hold functions. Here, a young Kevin Sullivan signs autographs for fans before a match in 1976.

Tony Altimore whispers last second advice to a then inexperienced Stan Hansen as the latter heads toward a match at the Field House. Altimore was capable as a wrestler, matchmaker, and manager, succeeding in all these areas.

Ivan Putski, a long-lasting World Wrestling Federation star, pounds Stan Hansen at the Field House. Hansen was one of the most hated wrestlers at the time due to breaking the neck of the beloved Bruno Sammartino and putting him out of action for some time.

Toro Mollando enters the ring at the Field House. Though known mainly in the New York area and Puerto Rico, he had a brief Ohio-Pennsylvania stint in the 1970s. The rotund villain did not win that many matches, but the people hated him regardless of his track record.

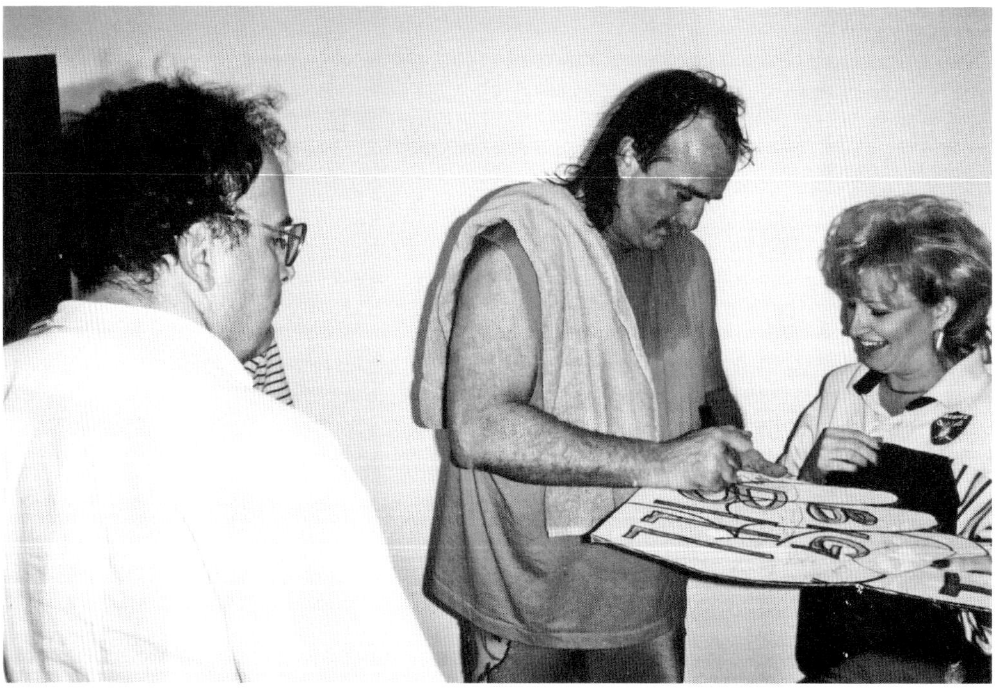

Jake "The Snake" Roberts remained a top name used by both big and small promotions in the Akron area following the armory years. Seen here signing autographs for fans, he was best known for bringing a live snake into the ring and for being a problem child, similar to Dr. Jerry Graham's behavior behind the scenes. (Courtesy Mike Lano.)

Frank Williams was a popular undercard wrestler on the Ohio-Pennsylvania circuit for years, though he lost more matches than he won. Cancer took him from this world. Though he wrestled in Columbus, Ohio, he saw much more action in Pennsylvania and New York.

Ricky Steamboat proved to be a major performer for both the World Wrestling Federation and World Championship Wrestling in the era following the armory's closing.

Though he pretended to be German in the tradition of Hans, Schmidt and Kurt Von Hess, Hans Mueller was actually a Midwesterner named Robert Colt, seen here in a 1981 Rubber Workers Union Hall match in Akron.

Scandor Akbar, who was shrugged off as an imitator of the Sheik and thus never given his chance at the Akron Armory, would outlive the Sheik, finding fame as a wrestler and manager on a national level. He passed away on August 20, 2010.

Though he started wrestling in 1947 and was a mainstay in Ohio for over two decades, Dr. Jerry Graham wore out his welcome and was considered too great a liability for any of the area promotions to use. Exiled to California, he continued to wrestle until 1992 because he had made and blown multiple fortunes. He is seen here (from left to right) in a 1991 group photograph with the Time Traveler, Johnny Legend, the Universal Playboy, Larry Ludden, and Steve Dalton in a Maywood, California, match where he was booked mainly for name value rather than what was left of his past talents. A series of strokes put him into a hospice, where he died in 1997. Known as one of wrestling's most bizarre characters, he left a legacy behind. "If you hear a story about Dr. Jerry Graham, it's true, no matter how absurd it sounds," once said Red Bastien. No one has ever disputed this statement. (Courtesy Ed Ahrens.)

After the armory closed, much of the old crew would continue working on a monthly basis at the Canton War Memorial Auditorium. Hank James, walking as slowly and arrogantly as ever, continues to annoy fans at this Canton show. When this promotion moved out, both the World Wrestling Federation and World Championship Wrestling would run there. An occasional show is still held at the arena by local groups.

Hank James leaves the ring at a much more hurried pace than he entered it to avoid boos, profanities, and an occasional popcorn box hurled at him by angry fans. In spite of this, James would hear cheers in his final Ohio endeavors as he did battle with people the audience hated even more than him.

Johnny Powers continued to work an occasional independent show in Ohio after the armory days before retiring to Canada, where, as of this writing, he still lives. Though always remembered as a fan favorite, Powers had a brief run as a villain managed by the hated Bobby Davis, complete with dyed blond hair. This earlier stage of his career is seldom mentioned.

Masonic lodges still indirectly supported wrestling shows in Northern and Central Ohio after the armory shut down, sometimes even renting their lodge halls and shrine temples to area promoters for spot shows.

"Mad Dog" Marcial Bovee (left), wrestling manager, booker, and occasional wrestler, speaks to bullfighter El Queretano while taking a break from a Mexican wrestling tour in Sonora. Mainly a West Coast figure, Bovee made his Ohio debut managing Hans Mueller in 1981 at the Rubber Workers Union Hall and promptly caused a riot that made the front of the *Beacon Journal* sports page but evidently got him released from the promotion as a liability after the riot. In 1982, he was back for the Jimmie Banks Memorial Show and caused a near riot again with Malcolm Monroe by his side. He did not come back until 1984 and again caused a riot in Logan, Ohio. In 1994, he was back in Lima for Al Snow's budding promotion, and in 2003, he returned to Akron on a regular basis under a new alias as the Time Traveler. For reasons well aware to some fans, he remains the author's favorite wrestling personality.

Shown here is a rare signed photograph of the late Eddie Gilbert, the son of Tommy Gilbert, nephew to the Masked Professional, and brother to Doug Gilbert. Like his other family members, Eddie proved a top draw in the East, Midwest, and Deep South. He died young in 1995.

King Tut of Pennsylvania made several appearances in Ohio for varied independent groups in the early 2000s, mainly feuding with fellow Pennsylvanian Powerhouse Hughes. Tut was a strong man himself and used a crushing bear hug to beat many men.

Denise Pierce, the author's wife, pets a cat before leaving for an Akron show. She enjoyed a brief career as a wrestling manager herself before leaving the trade in 1999.

Before moving on to much bigger and better things, Main Event Championship Wrestling operated in a reamed-out library in Massillon redubbed the Wrestleplex. Here, referee Earl Robinson speaks to fans before a Wrestleplex show.

Joe Rules was a mainstay among independents in New Jersey, fighting Hubie Volk, Rick Silver, and Dave Desire and occasionally drifting to the Akron-Cleveland area for a spot show. The high point of his career came when he, Kristy Kiss, Countess Noir, and other wrestlers appeared on *The Jerry Springer Show* and put on a performance as combative as any ring encounters.

Bounce, an Akron-based dance promoter and wrestling manager, put on an annual benefit show in Akron for several years, mainly featuring his star attraction, Big Animal, pictured here. Though Big Animal has since retired, Bounce still does an occasional show, sometimes even acting as a promoter for charity matches.

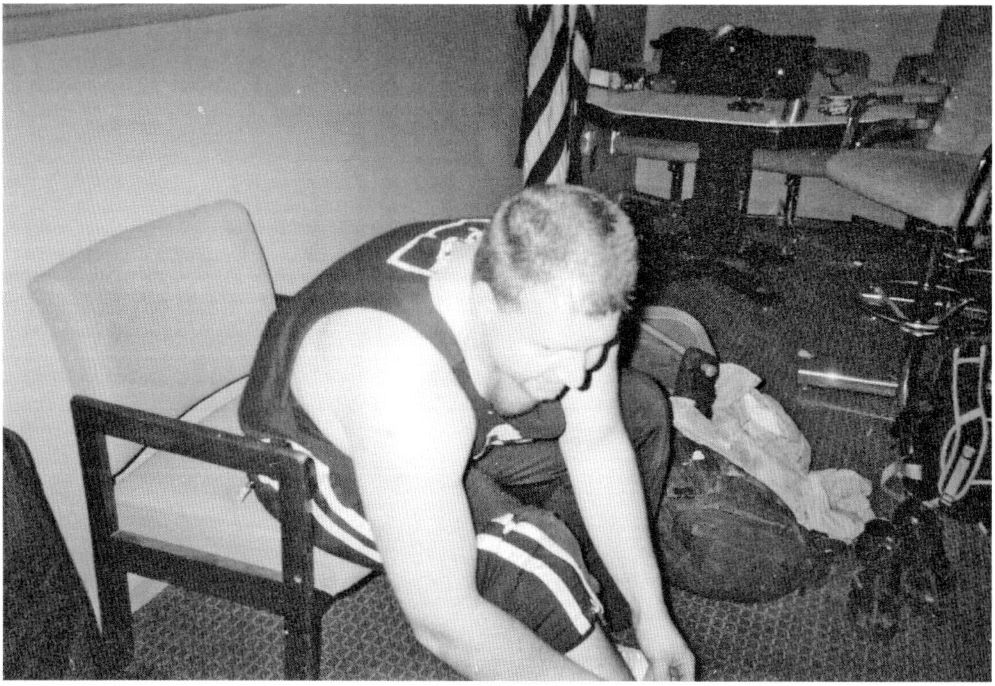

Jeff Cannon, a wrestler, trainer, and promoter of Ohio Championship Wrestling of Coshocton, has held an occasional show in the Akron suburbs but prefers to stick more toward his Central Ohio home base.

Virus, a masked wrestler from Chagrin Falls, Ohio, has appeared regularly for Mega Championship Wrestling, Ohio Championship Wrestling, Main Event Championship Wrestling, and the now defunct Cleveland All Pro Wrestling in recent years.

The Sheik, seen here choking Pampero Firpo with a wire hanger in a Canton bout after the close of the armory, continued to wrestle until he was in his 60s. He died from a stroke in 2003.

Sarah Lynn has become a favorite among fans of female wrestling in both Ohio and West Virginia, where she has been a regular on cards for many promotions. Her looks and ability have served to make her a big attraction with the fans.

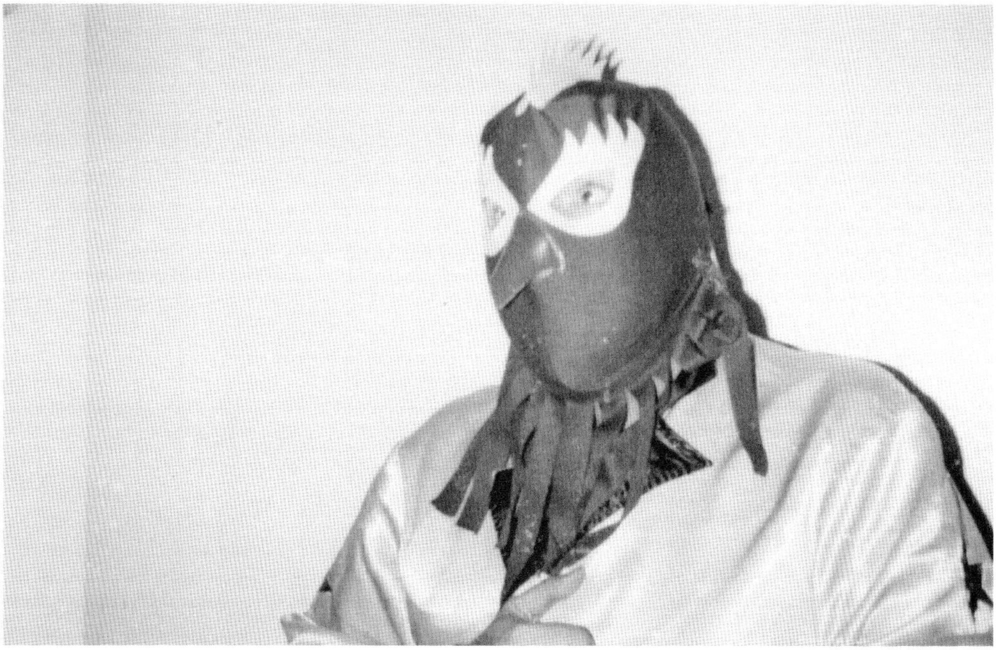

Mr. Cock-A-Doodle-Doo was another bizarre independent wrestler in a rooster mask, using such phrases as "Mr. Cock-A-Doodle-Doo is something to crow about," and "I will crush my opponents like broken eggs." He did not last long, in spite of a big publicity campaign, and retired.

Gary Fulton, also known as Charlie Fulton, was a reliable wrestler from Marion, Ohio, who was seen regularly in Akron and Canton from the 1970s into the 1980s. He appeared across the entire United States and, upon retirement, took to training other wrestlers.

The late wrestling reporter and photographer Robert Rothhaus poses with current Midwestern star Kaylee Pierce (no relation to the author). Pierce has since become a mainstay among women on the independent wrestling circuits around the globe.

Main Event Championship Wrestling introduced many new faces to the modern Akron area wrestling such as Danny Boy, seen here. Other graduates from the promotion's wrestling school include Christian Vaughn, Jebediah, Big Hurt, Wilbur Whitlock, Dick Jeremy, Shane Sensation, Justin Diaz, Nicky Skidds, Ron Reed, Larry Lavender, Supa Lucha, and Minka Murder.

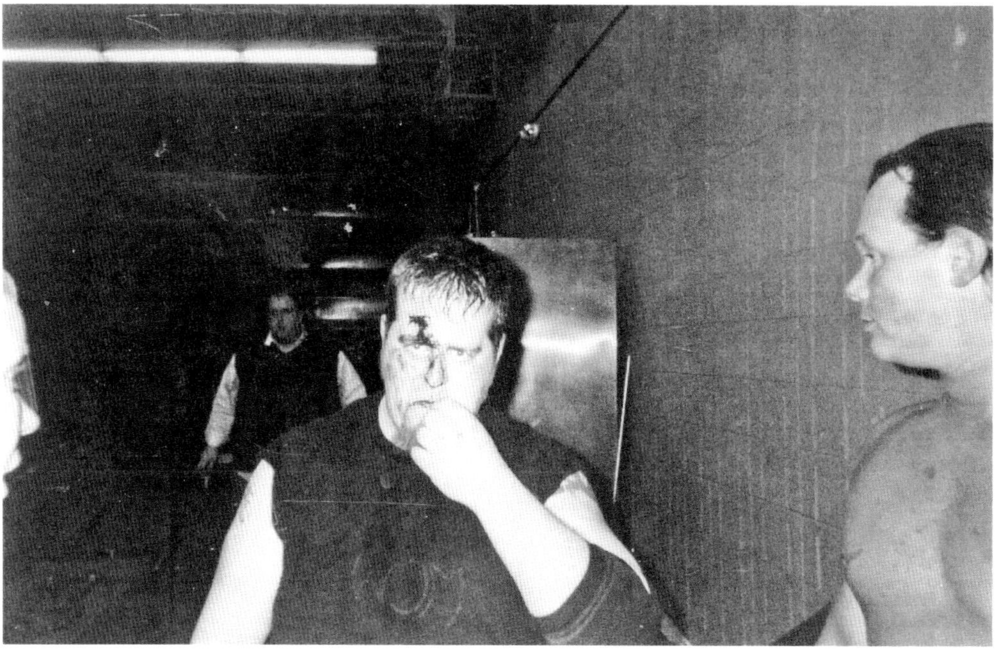

Chris Kole was one of the stars of Mega Championship Wrestling that focused and still places focus upon cards in Elyria (near Cleveland), but the promotion occasionally drifted into Akron suburbs for shows, while sending Kole and others to assorted promotions with which it had a working agreement.

Dark Star looked to be a bright and promising wrestler, but multiple injuries due to the extreme chances he took in the ring led to retirement. For a time, however, he wrestled many furious and frenzied matches against opponents such as Unknown and Virus.

The Navajo Warrior, a highly popular Native American grappler, made one swing through the Akron area in the late 1990s when promoter Jerry Gray made a sweep of the state. On this Ohio tour, he feuded with an eye-rolling rule-breaker, Toby "Mr. Insanity" Cline of Mansfield.

Brian O was a popular grappler in the Ohio–West Virginia area in the early 2000s. Usually, he wrestled as a single, but he occasionally teamed with David Flair, Ric Flair's son, of North Carolina.

In 1999, efforts were made to bring all-girl wrestling to Ohio with mixed results. This clip advertises a card for a wrestling extravaganza held in Medina, a half hour's drive from downtown Akron. The trend continues to this day with varied promotions running all-girl cards in assorted Ohio locations.

Jebediah poses before a match at the Shamrock Bar in Akron. Originally entering wrestling as an evil Amish grappler, he later abandoned this routine to become an outright villain and one of the best in indie circuits.

Cincinnati's Brian Pillman became a major star with both World Championship Wrestling and the World Wrestling Federation but did not live long enough to reach his full potential. A heart condition caused his passing while on a wrestling tour in Minnesota, when he was found dead in a Bloomington hotel room in 1997.

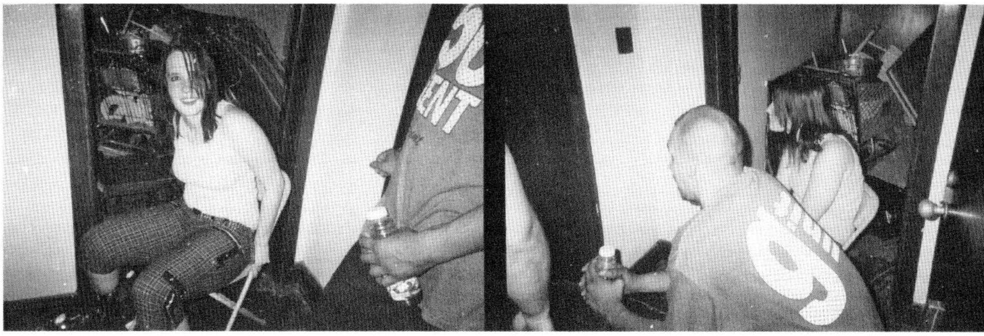

Jessicka Havok and Brandon X watch the action from the locker room at a Main Event Championship Wrestling card at a Knights of Columbus Hall in Akron. In recent years, Havok has become the subject of many magazine articles and publicity campaigns

Sin-D, as her ring name might imply, remains a beautiful woman wrestler, as well as an underhanded rule-breaker in the ring, continually working the Midwestern circuit. Though she has the looks to be a fan favorite, she prefers wrestling as a villain.

The vicious Don Kent continued to wrestle until 1986. He died from leukemia in 1993 and rests within the Memorial Park Cemetery in Battlecreek, Michigan, under his real name of Leo Smith.

The Psychopath was another Main Event Championship Wrestling graduate who appeared in the Akron-Canton area prior to retirement in 2007.

Ashley Nicely has remained a top woman wrestler on the Midwestern circuits, known for her looks, talent, and ability. She has also seen considerable action in the southern states in recent times.

In recent years, nostalgia conventions and wrestling reunions have become a big thing. Photographer Jeff Stoll signs an autograph book for a fan at a 1998 gathering in New Philadelphia, located an hour south of Akron.

Wrestling manager Slick Willie of Dayton was an interesting character. He is seen here with the author's wife, Denise Pierce, on a 1998 card in southern Ohio. Though he could have made the big time as he wanted, Willie was more interested in the restaurant business and retired after a few years of activity.

Referee Keith Smith, sometimes referred to as "Papa Smurf" behind his back due to his short stature, was nonetheless an authoritative arbitrator in the late 1990s and early 2000s. He, along with Logan Scott, Earl Robinson, David Young, and Jaime Starr, were some of the most consistently seen referees for a multitude of Ohio promotions.

In the 1990s, "Maniac" Mark Mustang (right) continued to portray a dangerous wrestling lunatic in the tradition of past mad men, such as the Sheik, Bull Curry, Abdullah the Butcher, and Tor Kamata.

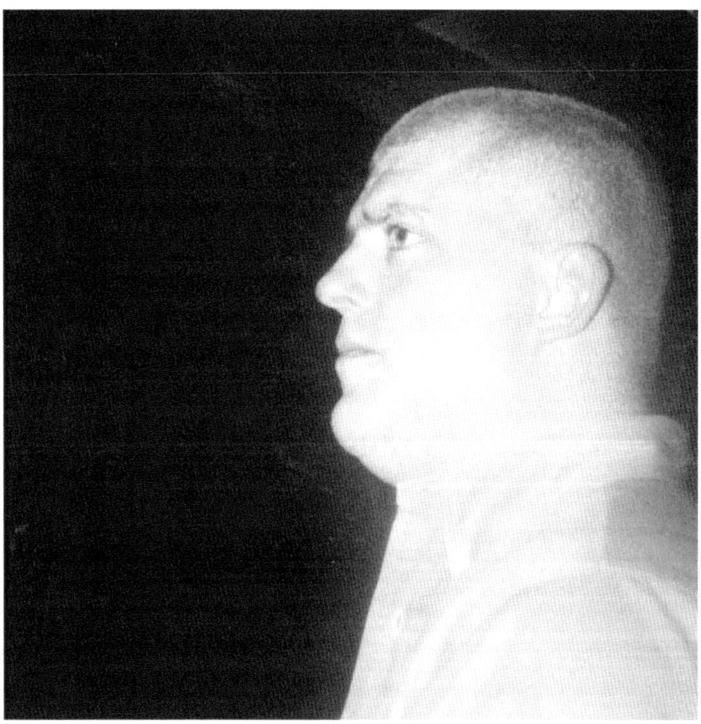

Gold Dust, seen here as plain old Dustin Rhodes arriving at the arena without his face paint, was a top draw for years when the World Wrestling Federation ran Ohio. In 2012, he made an appearance for an independent group in Massillon, Ohio.

Though the photograph is a bit off center, one can appreciate the difficulty "Irish" Mickey Doyle is in as he takes a hip toss from his opponent. Doyle, who wrestled out of Detroit, only had one or two matches at the Akron Armory but became a familiar Ohio face in a number of other towns and venues after the arena closed down.

From the late 1970s into the 1980s, Johnny Rivera was a popular wrestler with the fans, though he lost more than he won. At times, he obeyed the rules, and at other times, he broke them, depending on his opponent from show to show.

Billy Anderson wrestled amateur for Agua Fria High School out west in Arizona under his real name of Bill Laster. As a pro, he used the last name of Anderson and wrestled around the world. After retirement, he became an author, lecturer, Christian spokesman, and wrestling seminar coordinator, which includes varied stops in the Midwest even today. He has worked with and still works with seminars for amateurs in high school, going back to his amateur roots.

Often defined by his critics as looking like a walking bowling ball, Joe Joe Little was a capable wrestler in the Akron area in the early 2000s. He had especially bloody matches with rivals Jeff Cannon and G.Q. Status.

The Rootin-Tootin Buckaroos, two peculiar villains who have been on Main Event Championship Wrestling cards for years, look like something from a Sergio Leone Western, barring the masks with gunfighter mustaches sewn on. They have even gone so far as to insist these are not masks, but their real faces.

Stacy Marie has been a formidable female competitor for several years in Ohio and surrounding states, demonstrating a fast-paced style combined with great agility in the ring. No matter where she is booked, she gains great feedback from the critics and support from the fans.

Tim Collins of Uhrichsville produced the magazine *Turning Heel* as a privately printed venture. Publication ceased with the death of his coeditor, Randy Payton. These magazines are now considered rarities and are sought after by many collectors due to their limited run.

Pictured here is Billy Gunn of the Smoking Guns tag team along with his "brother" Bart Gunn when the WWF ran Northern Ohio in the early 1990s. Billy was considered a great attraction.

In recent times, a whole new wrestling crew has come to the Akron area, including Beastmaster, Bishop Slade, Tough Tina, Vinnie Violence, Christian Vaughn, Shawn Blaze, Cowboy Hughes, Seth Allen, Rhino, Mike Hercum, the Painkillers, Bill Martel, Sarah Danielle, Justin Mane, Pat Hayes, Ethan Wright, Krimson, Matt Mason, Benjamin Boone, Tommy Dreamer, Jason Bane, Johnny Gargano, Gregory Iron, Justin Diaz, Justin Sane, Bobby Beverly, Tony Banks, Robbie E, Al Snow, Tim Shady, Sassy Stephanie, Angel Dust, Matt Hardy, Virus, Wilbur Whitlock, Raptor, Eric Ryan, Doctor Lereaux, Aaron Maguire, Chris Daniels, Dick Jeremy, James Storm, G.Q. Status, Jimmy Lee, Supa Lucha, Sherman Tank, Truth Martini, Matt Cross, Reba Skye, Mr. Insanity, Malachi, Bull Miller, Nicky Skidds, Ian Decay, Hawaiian Lion, and Vincent Nothing. As the Book of Ecclesiastes in the Bible notes, one generation comes and another generation goes. In the future, who knows what other faces wait in the wings for their moment to come? Time marches on, and that is a certainty. Regardless, one thing may be relatively certain: professional wrestling in Akron will live on.

In the 1950s, Don Arnold of California was a big draw in Akron, Springfield, Columbus, and other towns on the circuit. He retired from wrestling in 1972 to live in a nudist colony near San Diego. In 1999, he wrote a booklet titled *Basic Nudism* about the naturist lifestyle. The inside cover signed by the wrestler-author is seen here. (Courtesy Alternative Publishing.)

4

THE AMATEURS

Amateur wrestling and professional wrestling are two different ball games. Competitive high school and junior college wrestling, however, have likewise been a major draw in Akron and the surrounding area, as has contests with the famed University of Akron and nearby Kent State.

At the high school level, Hoban, East, Ellet, Firestone, North, and Coventry have been some of the Akron schools to offer capable wrestling programs over the years, as have other area schools found in Medina, Kent, Cuyahoga Falls, Chagrin Falls, Copley, Sugarcreek, Canton, North Canton, New Philadelphia, Dennison, Twinsburg, Ravenna, Dover, Massillon, Hudson, Alliance, Wooster, and Aurora.

Varied junior colleges have produced state and national champions at their competitive level, while the University of Akron downtown thrives with many sports.

Training camps, private wrestling clubs, and self-defense schools also supplement schooling for wrestlers, again making it a popular sport at both an individual and team level.

Amateur wrestling varies greatly from the professional style. There is no showboating or acting. The combatants wear headgear and hold an opponent down for a count of one rather than three to win a match. Rules are strictly enforced, and wrestlers are evenly matched by weight. Though the differences are like night and day, interest in both forms of wrestling often overlap. Many high school and collegiate wrestlers also went on to great professional careers, including Vern Gagne, Kurt Angle, Chris Taylor, Danny Hodge, and Dick Hutton.

Young wrestlers attend a clinic to learn the moves at an Akron wrestling seminar. Here, they watch the art of a stand out and escape, two of the basics of amateur wrestling.

The late Kerry Von Erich was a big hero to wrestling fans in Northern Ohio in the 1990s, but he could not conquer a motorcycle accident that led to the amputation of a foot, a secret he kept from others on the trade. Though he wrestled with an artificial limb and showered with his boots on, he grew addicted to painkillers and shot himself. Von Erich was an outstanding high school athlete in Texas before turning professional; he toured not only Ohio but the world.

An unidentified assistant coach from the 1980s attends a seeding meeting. Seeding sessions place the wrestlers with the best records in opposite brackets so they do not fight each other until the finals. Sometimes it works out and sometimes there are upsets.

Ellet High School, situated on the east side of Akron, has offered an effective wrestling program for several years. The school is one of many in Akron known for both successful academics and sports. (Courtesy Summit County Library.)

The University of Akron has likewise featured some great amateur wrestlers. National championships have been held there as well. (Courtesy Summit County Library.)

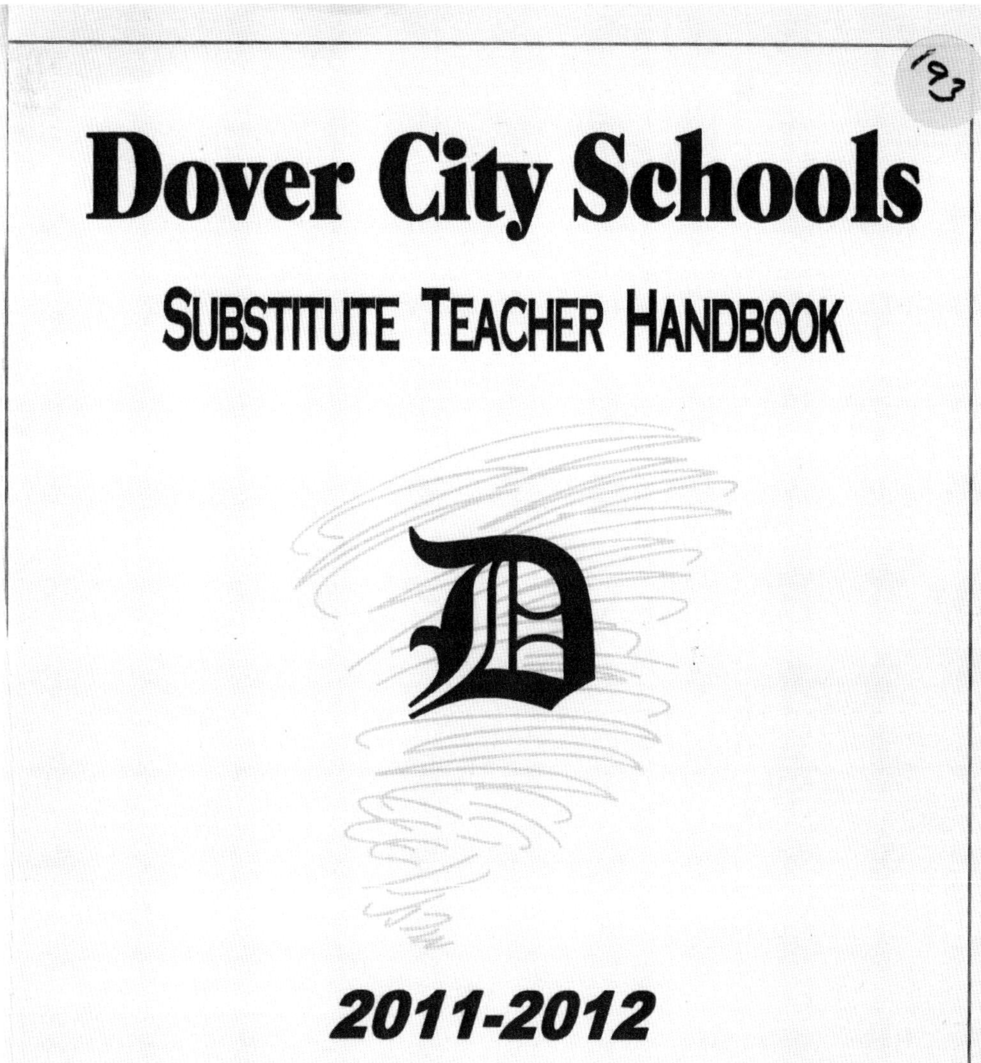
Dover City Schools

SUBSTITUTE TEACHER HANDBOOK

2011-2012

Addressing Tomorrow's
Challenges Today!

Shown here is the cover of a substitute teacher handbook for Dover High School, located below Akron. Like most schools, Dover's wrestling, basketball, football, and other sports have seen ups and downs, with some so-so years intertwined with truly outstanding seasons. The high school also housed at least one pro wrestling show in the early 1970s; it was held in the gym as a fundraiser.

Still happy about his seeding picks, this unidentified coach again smiles for the camera before an amateur tournament.

Booster clubs have long been a part of high school wrestling, with friends and family cheering from the stands, arranging post-match parties, or forming caravans to important tournaments. Here, two unidentified wrestling lovers socialize at a booster club party in an Akron restaurant following a state tournament.

VARSITY WRESTLING

DECEMBER			
Wed	5	Triway/West Holmes/NW	5:00
Sat	8	at Marysville Duals	10:00
Sat	15	Tri w/ Timken/Northmor	11:00
Wed	19	Tri w/Indian Valley/Orrville	6:00
Sat	22	at Claymont w/Solon	6:00
Sat	29	at Cardington Dual	10:00
JANUARY			
Fri	4	at STICHCO Classic	4:00
Sat	5	at STICHCO Classic	11:00
Fri	11	at Marion Elgin Invite	4:30
Sat	12	at Marion Elgin Invite	10:00
Sat	19	Waynedale Duals	9:00
Wed	23	Regional Quarter State Duals	TBA
Sat	26	at Joe Szymczak Duals	9:00
FEBRUARY			
Sat	2	at Smithville WCAL Champ	TBA
Fri	15	at Northwestern Sectional	TBA
Sat	16	at Northwestern Sectional	TBA
Fri	22	at Garfield Heights District	TBA
Sat	23	at Garfield Heights District	TBA
Thu	28	State Tournament at OSU	TBA
MARCH			
Fri	1	State Tournament at OSU	TBA
Sat	2	State Tournament at OSU	TBA

GIRLS VARSITY/JV BASKETBALL

NOVEMBER			
Sat	24	Tuslaw	7:30
Thu	29	Chippewa	7:30
DECEMBER			
Thu	6	at Smithville	7:30
Sat	8	at Central Christian	2:30
Thu	13	at Rittman	7:30
Wed	19	at Canton South	7:30
Thu	20	Hillsdale	7:30
Thu	27	Norwayne	7:30
Sat	29	Tuscarawas C.C. Varsity only	1:00
JANUARY			
Thu	3	Dalton	7:30
Thu	10	at Northwestern	7:30
Sat	12	at Chippewa	7:30
Thu	17	Smithville	7:30
Sat	19	at Field	2:30
Thu	24	Rittman	7:30
Sat	26	at Hillsdale	2:30
Thu	31	at Norwayne	7:30
FEBRUARY			
Sat	2	Northwest	2:30
Thu	7	at Dalton	7:30
Sat	9	at Triway	2:30
Tue	12	Northwestern	7:30
Thu	14	Loudonville	7:30

JV games start 1 1/2 hrs before varsity

BOYS FRESHMAN BASKETBAL

DECEMBER			
Sat	1	at Chippewa	10:
Thu	6	Smithville	6:
Mon	10	at Hiland	6:
Thu	13	Rittman	6:
Sat	15	Akron Ellet at Edgewood Comm. Ctr N. Can	12:
Thu	20	at Hillsdale	6:
Sat	22	Tuslaw	10:
Thu	27	at Norwayne	6:
JANUARY			
Thu	3	at Dalton	6:
Sat	12	Chippewa	10:
Thu	17	at Smithville	6:
Tue	22	at CantonCentral Cath	5:
Thu	24	at Rittman	6:
Sat	26	Hillsdale	10:
Thu	31	Norwayne	6:
FEBRUARY			
Thu	7	Dalton	6:

This contemporary schedule for Waynedale High School depicts a well-rounded schedule of meets and tournaments before the big state tournament at Ohio State University. Waynedale is a small school but has produced some outstanding wrestling talent.

Farm towns such as Sugarcreek and Dover, both located below Akron, have always offered stiff wrestling competitors. This photograph depicts two Garaway varsity wrestling groups in Sugarcreek during a practice session.

Here is another practice session photograph from Garaway taken several seasons ago, where, again, two lighter-weight amateurs struggle to gain the upper hand on each other. Practices, of course, are designed for the young wrestlers to enhance their skills but can often be grueling events on their own.

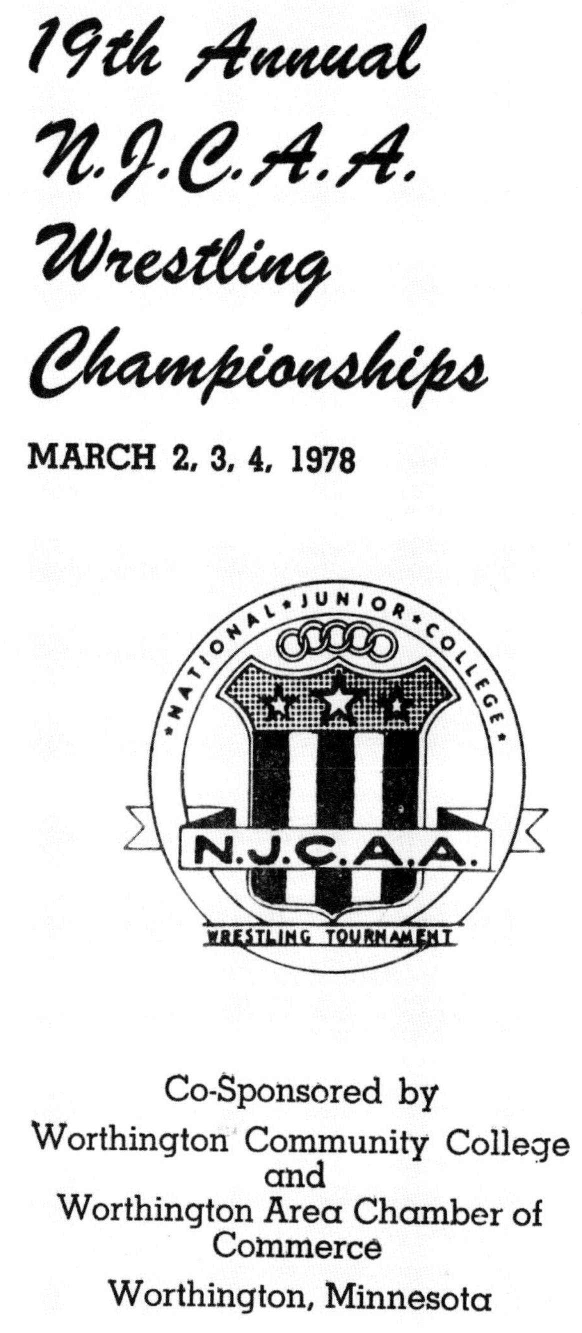

19th Annual N.J.C.A.A. Wrestling Championships

MARCH 2, 3, 4, 1978

NATIONAL • JUNIOR • COLLEGE

N.J.C.A.A.

WRESTLING TOURNAMENT

Co-Sponsored by
Worthington Community College
and
Worthington Area Chamber of Commerce
Worthington, Minnesota

Shown here is a flyer for the 1978 National Junior College Wrestling Tournament in Worthington, Minnesota, in which Ohio community colleges were well represented. Greg Byrne of Lakeland Community College of Mentor won first place in the heavyweight division, and Charles Hageman of Cuyahoga West Community College in Parma took second in the 190-pound weight class, bringing honor to both schools north of Akron. The tournament was marred by a tremendous snowstorm that left many teams and spectators stranded in Worthington during and after the tournament.

Looking more like a pack of ruffians than athletes, a group of collegiate wrestlers pose outside a local gymnasium in Akron. Curiously, note the pipes in the mouths of some of the grapplers, indicating a time before smoking was considered harmful and non-athletic.

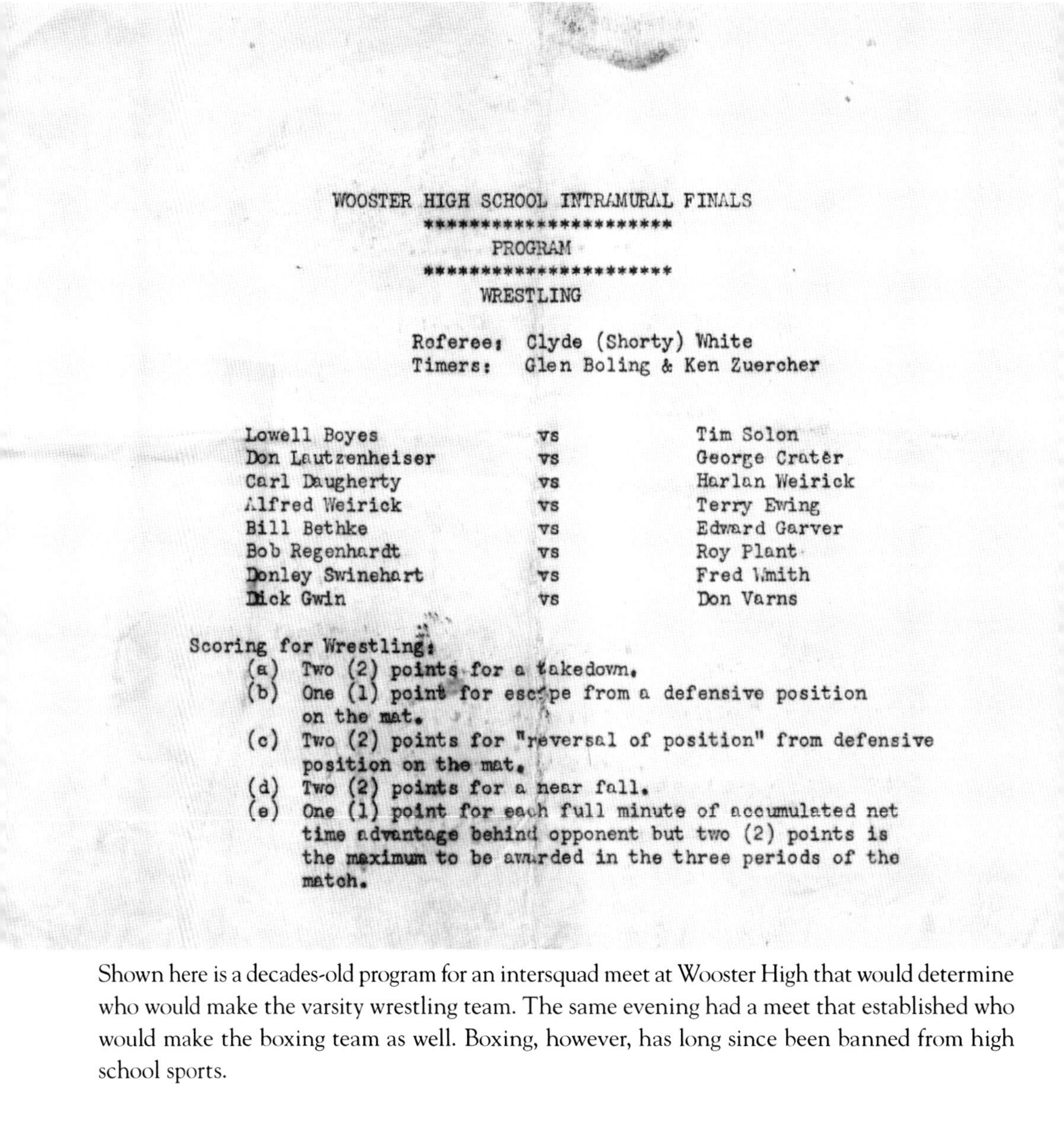

WOOSTER HIGH SCHOOL INTRAMURAL FINALS
****
PROGRAM
****
WRESTLING

Referee: Clyde (Shorty) White
Timers: Glen Boling & Ken Zuercher

Lowell Boyes	vs	Tim Solon
Don Lautzenheiser	vs	George Crater
Carl Daugherty	vs	Harlan Weirick
Alfred Weirick	vs	Terry Ewing
Bill Bethke	vs	Edward Garver
Bob Regenhardt	vs	Roy Plant
Donley Swinehart	vs	Fred Wmith
Dick Gwin	vs	Don Varns

Scoring for Wrestling:

(a) Two (2) points for a takedown.
(b) One (1) point for escape from a defensive position on the mat.
(c) Two (2) points for "reversal of position" from defensive position on the mat.
(d) Two (2) points for a near fall.
(e) One (1) point for each full minute of accumulated net time advantage behind opponent but two (2) points is the maximum to be awarded in the three periods of the match.

Shown here is a decades-old program for an intersquad meet at Wooster High that would determine who would make the varsity wrestling team. The same evening had a meet that established who would make the boxing team as well. Boxing, however, has long since been banned from high school sports.

Be it an amateur division or the more elaborate professionals, wrestling has, is, and always will be a part of Akron and surrounding areas. History has lived, lives, and will continue to live in the world of grips, grunts, and groans.